Ideas in Progress
Marxism and Radical Social Thought

Ideas in Progress

Larry Portis

Georges Sorel

Pluto Press

First published 1980 by Pluto Press Limited,
Unit 10 Spencer Court, 7 Chalcot Road, London NW1 8LH
Copyright © Larry Portis 1980
ISBN 0 86104 303 0
Photoset by Photobooks (Bristol) Limited,
28/30 Midland Road, St Philips, Bristol
Printed in Great Britain by
The Camelot Press Limited, Southampton

Contents

Introduction / 1

1. The Situation of Georges Sorel / 4

2. Marxism and Bourgeois Sociology:
   The Analytical Poles of Class Conflict / 19

3. The Politics of Class Struggle: Against the
   Reproduction of Capitalist Polity / 43

4. The Revolutionary *Syndicats* and the General Strike / 64

5. 'Embourgeoisement': The Politics of
   Culture in the Era of Monopoly Capitalism / 88

Epilogue / 108

References / 113

To Bruce and Nora Portis

Acknowledgements

It is with fondness and gratitude that I thank David L. Clark and Christiane Passevent for helping me with the manuscript. Special regards to Mydia.

Introduction

One of the great difficulties associated with the contemporary renaissance of marxist studies and practice has been the determination of proper historical antecedents. 'Marxism' has almost become a scholastic discipline as commentators remain preoccupied with qualifying or disputing the veracity of other commentators – other marxists. The texts of the master are now pored over and hotly debated: Was Marx consistent? What was his philosophical touchstone? What would he have done in the present situation? The hagiography now extends to the second and third generations of marxists: Plekhanov, Lenin, Trotsky, Luxemburg, Gramsci, Lukacs.

In an important sense this intense interest in revolutionary theory represents the maturing of what used to be called the 'New Left'. Much of the emotional content of the 'counter-cultural' and political movements of the 1960s and early 70s has given way to a more rational and profound approach to social change, an approach which necessarily involves a discovery of marxism. Through this sometimes blind sifting of revolutionary thought will undoubtedly come new syntheses, new perspectives on revolutionary tactics and new insights into the meaning of social revolution.

Today's marxist revolutionaries are perhaps at times confused by the myriad of directions open to them and by the distorted configurations of existing 'socialist' societies, but they have an unprecedented historical opportunity to learn from over a hundred years of revolutionary practice. In a way they have a range of ideological choice which preceding generations did not enjoy. And it is because of these new historical conditions that there is renewed interest in the work of Georges Sorel.

It was Sorel who produced the most profound and extensive body of marxist analysis to appear in France until the post

1

World War Two era when Jean-Paul Sartre, Henri Lefebvre, Louis Althusser and Nicos Poulantzas revitalised French marxism. Sorel was the first French marxist to react strongly against the mechanical determinism which was both a symptom and a cause of an unimaginative and sterile socialist *praxis*. In the process, he explored the philosophical foundations of Marx's thought and elaborated how Hegel's influence upon the former militated against the superficial determinism that French socialists everywhere were content with. The so-called 'hegelian revival' which developed in Europe during the first part of the twentieth century was driven by just this consideration. On a less abstract level, Sorel was preoccupied with the question of proletarian consciousness, for he knew that no amount of political organisation could result in a proletarian revolution if the workers were not psychologically – ideologically – ready to structure their own lives according to new principles of human conduct and morality. It was a question of determining exactly what a generalised revolutionary proletarian consciousness was and how it could develop.

For Sorel, this question of revolutionary proletarian consciousness was the acid test of revolutionary strategy and tactics. To assume any other priority was to deviate from the road to revolution onto some reformist path that would ultimately facilitate the functioning of capitalism itself. From his position outside the organised structure of the French socialist movement, Sorel acted as a sort of revolutionary gadfly, uncompromising in attacking simplistic thinking and opportunism wherever he found it. In doing this, he allied with the revolutionary syndicalist movement which emerged during the middle years of the 1890s. But Sorel did not wish to play an organising or administrative role in the movement. The role he played, and it was a considerable one in terms of its influence on the revolutionaries of his time, was that of the true revolutionary intellectual – the person who applies his or her peculiar facility with analytical expression to a revolutionary movement, without thought of personal gain.

The questions of revolutionary analysis and strategy which Sorel struggled with decades ago have not been resolved to this day. If anything they have been made more nuanced and obscure,

2

not only by the efforts of bourgeois ideologists inside and outside the universities, but by the mechanism of capitalist development itself. It is thus an important part of the revolutionary process to return continually to the relative beginnings of the struggle – to pose, over and over again, the basic questions, to separate the essential from the secondary. Georges Sorel has no precise solutions to offer us, but understanding how he coped with the questions with which we are still preoccupied clarifies a social process which is as much ours as it was his. Thus, the purpose of this book is to address the most essential questions of revolutionary thought and action, and to explain how they were shaped by contingencies of time and place.

1. The Situation of Georges Sorel

The life of Georges Sorel (1847-1922) spans the period during which French society became modern – that is, when it was transformed by capitalist industry into a democratic polity. The Revolution of 1848 exploded a year after his birth, at once expressing the need of middle and petty-bourgeois classes for a liberalised economic environment, and the dim but growing comprehension of the working classes of their ever-increasing vulnerability and need for collective defence. But he grew up during a period of reaction, the twenty year rule of Louis Napoleon Bonaparte (1851-71), a time when the 'grand-bourgeoisie' of finance laid the foundations of modern industrial capitalism in France – railroads, mining, banking and communications. It was a long night for the French working class, which was only briefly illuminated by the lightning rise of revolutionary urban communes in the immediate wake of the French defeat in the Franco-Prussian War. Even after the establishment of the Third French Republic in 1871 the reaction continued. The bloody massacres of the communards merely gave way to a general policy of keeping the working class in check by means of physical and legal repression. Labour organisation itself was illegal until 1884.

But if French society seemed to be stable during these years, much was happening beneath the rigid political crust, developments which would soon crack things wide open. Industrialisation was advancing rapidly; steel, chemicals and heavy manufacturing accelerated a shift of the population to urban centres. With the check of a rightist attempt to re-establish a form of autocratic government in 1876 (the 'Seize Mai' of General McMahon), the free-for-all of parliamentary government initiated a political buoyancy that saw increasing socialist involvement. In addition, the return of amnestied communards

4

and the legalisation of labour organisation in the 1880s contributed to a rise of working-class militancy and strikes. But the early years of the organised labour movement in France saw this new form of social organisation dominated by the fledgling socialist organisations. It was not until the early years of the 1890s that an autonomous working-class movement existed along with all the other elements which constitute the politics and social conflicts of today. Most important, the *Bourses du Travail*, labour exchanges organised and controlled by the workers were formed in 1892; and the General Confederation of Labour (*Confédération Générale de Travail*, or C.G.T.), a militant federation of labour unions independent of political control, was formed in 1895.

Because Sorel turned his active attention to the social movement in 1892 – just when the socio-political context achieved its modern aspect – his observations and analyses continue to strike to the essentials of our present experience. Reformist versus revolutionary socialist parties, the conflict between democratic centralism and forms of anarchist-style federalism, movements of working-class autonomy, terrorism, and revolutionary sectarianism: the existence of all these elements prevented Sorel from developing a utopian socialist perspective. The dynamic of revolutionary struggle had become too rich, too complex, and too rooted in practical reality to support the millenarianism or utopianism of previous generations. From this time on it was only opportunism or analytical sterility which would support deterministic considerations of the struggle. The role of Sorel would be to oppose such regressive tendencies within the movement.

For a period of thirty years, from 1892 to 1922 when he died, Sorel attempted, through books, articles, lectures and informal contacts with young revolutionaries, to clarify the course of social struggle in France and to determine how the proletariat might best develop its revolutionary capacity. As a spokesman for a marxism characterised by its stress upon the necessity for autonomous proletarian action in the revolutionary struggle, Sorel's influence, however unacknowledged, is still being felt today.

But who was Georges Sorel? And how did he become a

marxist important to us? First, he was an alienated individual in a very modern sense. He was born into a family that could easily be called bourgeois, given that his father was the director of a business concern and his mother the daughter of an army officer. But these facts must be qualified by noting that if his father was a petty capitalist, he was not a successful one, and his chronic financial straits must have coloured Sorel's eventual view of capitalist social relations. At any rate, it may have encouraged him to seek the security of state employment by obtaining a diploma from the École Polytechnique, the state technical school, and securing a position with the Department of Roads and Bridges. Sorel began this work in 1867, at the age of 20, and his youth and social background can only remind us that the state civil service is as much the refuge of petty-bourgeois victims of the capitalist competitive dynamic as it is for the more upwardly mobile.

In Sorel's case these biographical details are especially important when we consider his mature political attitudes and social analysis, because the latter emerged fairly late in his life and without *apparent* foundation. Once in the state engineering corps, Sorel was effectively removed from modern France. From 1867 to 1871, spanning the events of the Franco-Prussian War and the Commune, he worked in Corsica, an island whose remoteness must have been particularly felt one hundred years ago. Then, in 1871, he was transferred to the southern village of Albi, then to Gap in the same region, then to Algeria for three years, and eventually to Perpignan where he worked from 1879 to his retirement in 1892. During this time he produced no social theory, no analyses of capitalist development, no reflections on proletarian revolution – only a couple of articles on the French Revolution which appeared just before his retirement from the state service.

So how could twenty-five years of virtual isolation from French life produce a major contributor to marxist analysis? In answering the question, the psychological mechanism which led Sorel to break with the life of his social class must be described. For some reason Sorel was not content to live as a state engineer removed to the periphery of French culture, although he accepted his situation as necessary. After all, what else was there for a young man without financial resources or a taste for entre-preneurship, especially at a time of political reaction?

In a way Sorel had been plucked out of modern French life and removed from the necessity to make personal compromises at the very moment he entered adulthood. Living in the wild provinces of southern France and the colonial atmospheres of Algeria and Corsica kept something intact in Sorel that the pressures of mature life quickly remove from most petty bour-geois. His youthful naïveté was not shattered by the necessity to connive his way to personal success; his intellectual openness was not sealed-over by the necessity to conform to a 'practical' conventional wisdom; and he was not constrained to affect an urban sophistication in order to facilitate his social acceptance. But what did he miss? If Sorel's twenty-five years outside the social mainstream preserved something vital in him, what did he feel lacking? What frustrations did it bring which could ultimately turn his mind to questions of social development and politics?

Isolation is important in intellectual development. The *habit* of at least attempting to view the world objectively is born of an alienation from the environment, in some form, in every intellectual. Sorel was well-educated, and educated in a practical way, as opposed to the idealist education received by students of the time who followed a more literary or philosophical line of study. He was capable of following the shocking events of his time – the fall of the Second Empire, the establishment of the Communes, their subsequent brutal repression, and the political opportunism which ushered in the Third Republic; but he could not, or at least did not, participate in these events. Very likely, as he surveyed along a dirt road among the romantic crags of Corsica, or rested in a furnished room after a day in the plains of Algeria, he felt that events were passing him by.

Social perspectives are not formed completely by exposure to certain ideas, nor are they given specific content by general social origins. In Sorel, up to this point, I have discussed the son of an unsuccessful petty-capitalist manager who was undoubt-edly pushed into a safe occupational position by a family who wished to spare him the insecurities they had experienced. It was a successful move. Sorel led, from the beginning, an occupation-ally, financially and socially secure existence. But his family could do nothing to ameliorate the ontological insecurity which was encouraged during every phase of his life. The need to settle in order to escape the fate of his father meant that his life was a perpetual retreat socially as well as, fate had it, geographically.

In this isolation, Sorel was completely alone for eight years, until 1875, when he began living with a chamber maid who had cared for him in an hotel in Lyon when he was ill. It was said later by Sorel's relatives that this woman, Marie David, while not a 'political person' in the sense that most modern intellectuals consider someone to be 'politicised', was nevertheless intelligent and outspoken in her devotion to the 'people' and her hatred of injustice. If Sorel was in Corsica during the terrible year of 1871, Marie David was probably in Lyon, where a Commune was established and where revolutionary fervour ran deep. Here was the catalyst which could have sparked the development of a critical revolutionary perspective – a social and intellectual alienation being fed by an emotional influence informed by first hand observation. Sorel always referred to his companion (although together twenty years they were never married) as a source of tremendous inspiration for his work. And perhaps it is significant that his political position itself followed a model of encouraging an emotional, a 'moral', involvement in social struggle without becoming interested in politics as a thing in itself.

In 1892 Sorel's life changed abruptly, and by his own volition. In that year he resigned from the civil service after having been awarded the Legion of Honour the previous year (automatic in the case of such seniority and impending retirement) and having been made Chief Engineer. So Sorel, at the young age of forty-five, could settle into his retirement after exactly twenty-five years of service. Yet, there was one remarkable aspect of this early retirement: Sorel refused a government pension that he had earned and could have had until his death. Years later he explained that in doing so he simply wished not to be compromised in any way. It can only be concluded that the change in his life had been methodically planned, and that the intensive study of social dynamics upon which he embarked soon after his installation in Paris in 1892 represented the fulfilment of a long-standing dream.

Thus Sorel's first life, before his emergence on the French political scene, was not exactly typical of his social class; it was not classically bourgeois as many commentators have claimed. The man had analytical talents which were not freely expressed in either his work or his cultural milieu; and rather than conform – have children, strive for social respectability, accept an orthodox life of work and retirement – he planned and executed a radical break which suddenly allowed him to pour all his energy into political dialogue and social analysis. A solitary man with a strong will, but without experience or contacts within the socialist and working-class movements, his rapid emergence as the most profound of French marxist analysts before World War One should be an inspiration to all who desire to break with and combat capitalism.

Sorel's commitment to the proletarian movement took on clarity only gradually. For a period of five or six years following his move to Paris in 1892, he gave close attention to all developments in social theory, whether of a marxist or a strictly academic nature. He haunted the Sorbonne and quickly became familiar with the major figures in the budding field of 'sociology'. For example, he attended Émile Durkheim's defence of his doctoral dissertation in 1893, and during the next two years he published critiques of Durkheim, Gabriel Tarde, Gustave LeBon and Cesare Lombroso. Thus he acquainted himself with the sociologies of education, crowds, suggestion, prisons and virtually every other aspect of non-marxist social theory. Once he had assimilated the principles of academic sociological thought he ceased to consider these principles strictly on their own terms. Rather, he concentrated upon their political implications and he refused to engage in academic, philosophical debates concerning them. Hereafter he dealt with the notions and idea systems of academic sociology only in tactical terms, from a revolutionary socialist perspective.

Sorel's involvement with marxism also began within a year of his arrival in Paris. Naturally he did not immediately begin to make critical contributions to it. But in 1893 and 1894 he began publishing articles, and even a letter to the editor of an academic journal, vaunting the importance of Karl Marx's work. In 1894 he contributed heavily to *L'Ère nouvelle*, the first French journal

9

devoted to marxist philosophy and analysis. Sorel noted at this time that Marx was not studied at all in scholarly circles, although his thought represented 'the greatest philosophical breakthrough to have occurred in several centuries; it marks the point of departure for an unlimited transformation in our thinking. Today all our ideas must centre around the new principles stemming from scientific socialism.'[1] *L'Ère nouvelle* was published for only seventeen months, but it allowed the first appearance in France of many of the most important marxist texts, including those of Marx, Engels, Kautsky, and Plekhanov.

In 1895, Sorel, along with Paul Lafargue (Marx's son-in-law), Paul Bonnet (a founder of *L'Ère nouvelle*), and Georges Deville (who first translated Marx's *Capital* into French), founded a new journal, *Le Devenir social* ('The Social Process'), which continued the same work on a broader and more sophisticated level. In November 1895, in one of the first numbers of *Le Devenir social*, Sorel published a long review article, 'Superstition socialiste?', in which he articulated positions he would maintain fairly intact throughout the rest of his life. On the theoretical level he attempted to remove marxism entirely from the 'organic' versus 'mechanical' frame of reference – a general conception which had captivated the academic sociologists. 'Marxists', he said, 'do not draw a distinction between natural or legitimate social institutions and artificial or oppressive ones.'[2] He pointed out that the organic-mechanical dichotomy is a distinction which is rather characteristic of a bourgeois moral outlook in that it legitimises certain institutions, those that maintain bourgeois control, while condemning socially subversive tendencies as being 'abnormal'.

Sorel also attempted to remove marxism from the sort of anthropomorphic thinking that was typical of bourgeois thought in the nineteenth century. Historical materialism, he wrote, was an advance in human thought precisely because it stripped the veil of idealist mystification from our socio-historical gaze. 'Capitalism doesn't have a *will*, a *spirit*, which is reflective of its *essence*. Capitalism is a word and nothing more; what has force and will is the individual working within a system of economic and social relations proper to an historical era characterised by the high functioning of capitalism.'[3] Thus, rather than a 'thing'

10

moving through history, capitalism is merely a name given to a certain complex of socio-economic relations, or, one could say equally, a certain mode of production. The same logic should be applied when considering political structures. In 1895, when the outlook of the socialist movement was still by and large expressed in revolutionary terms, there existed no tortured social-democratic rationale for 'seizing state power' as a prelude to social revolution, or giving active support to state welfare projects designed to co-opt or dampen the class struggle. Sorel felt himself to be on fairly sure and uncontroversial ground in saying that 'one of the outstanding tasks of the proletariat is, obviously, to combat with every possible means the extension of the state and to free social life from the intervention of state functionaries. Statism is the ideal of the petty bourgeoisie; it is the exact opposite of socialism.'[4]

It was indeed a period when the French state was extending its influence and fortifying its institutions. In response to a combination of socialist electoral successes, a mounting wave of strikes, and a good two years of anarchist terror – all of which took place simultaneously (1892-94) – the French political system reacted almost instinctively to protect itself. The terrorism elicited expanded police powers and restrictions on civil liberties, but the strikes brought forth government arbitration between capital and labour as well as ameliorative programmes of social welfare. The events also stimulated bourgeois political factions to coalesce into more solid alliances and eventually into political parties of the modern sort. The outstanding political events of the period 1895–1905 figured centrally in this multi-faceted reaction of the state to what constituted a growing revolutionary opposition.

Specifically, the celebrated Dreyfus Affair, wherein the progressive bourgeoisie and segments of the socialist movement rallied to defend Alfred Dreyfus, an army officer unjustly accused and convicted of handing secret service documents to the Germans, served as an ideological vehicle of party formation. The Dreyfus Affair helped to propel a more progressive bourgeois government to power in 1898; and a campaign to separate church from state served the same function in the elections of 1902. The fact that socialists participated in these campaigns meant that

11

certain questions of revolutionary tactics were posed with practical seriousness: how to maintain and encourage the development of revolutionary proletarian consciousness in the face of compelling bourgeois political campaigns? What should be the role of electoral politics in the revolutionary class struggle? How was the development of state institutions and sophisticated methods of ideological formation presenting new problems for the revolutionary movement?

From the mid-1890s until his death in 1922, Sorel applied marxist analysis to these essential questions and others, such as the role of education in French social and political life, the foundations of economic value from a marxist perspective, and changes within French political life. His stress upon the ideological dynamic of the revolutionary process, both within the proletariat and the bourgeoisie, distinguished his marxism sharply from the reigning economic determinism.

Sorel's marxism was already at a high level of sophistication by the end of the century, extending to a serious consideration of the hegelian elements existing within Marx's thought and to the dialectic itself, which Sorel virtually had to unearth and reconstruct from the suggestions of it to be found in the few texts then available to French readers. Of course the problem of divining the dialectical method was as great for everyone at this time, given the fact that the philosophically explicit early writings of Marx were entirely unknown. Sorel's passing interest in Henri Bergson's attempts to go beyond the conceptual limitations of the reigning positivism into the realm of time, duration, flux and symbiosis was reflective of his search for the philosophical underpinnings of Marx's work.

Eventually, in *Reflections on Violence* (1908), Sorel attempted to label the method by which one could isolate an object of socio-historical analysis in order to determine its qualitative nature in the context of its multi-variate relations with other phenomena – '*diremption*', he called it. It was one of the few times that he left the realm of the analytical and philosophical and entered the swampy regions of the 'theoretical'. Nevertheless, the attention he gave to attempting to understand and define the perception of dialectical historical development and the 'dialectical method' was important in terms of represent-

12

ing a contribution to marxist philosophy, and in terms of his influence on other marxists. Antonio Gramsci, for example, long after his imprisonment and active political involvement, advised that 'It is certainly necessary to study Sorel in order to grasp what is most essential and permanent, underneath the confusing encrustations with which intellectual and dilettante admirers have covered his thought.'[5] Gramsci thus expressed the opinion that prevailed after the turn of the century: that Sorel was the French Plekhanov or Labriola – the single individual most responsible for the development of marxism in his native country.

Most of what has been written on the subject of Georges Sorel is confusing, especially if the widely differing interpretations of his thought are compared. The great majority of these studies have been written by academic writers in search of a relatively unworked field; or, alternatively, Sorel has figured in some idealist attempt to abstract 'meta-historical' tendencies out of social history.[6]

Attention given to Sorel in the anglo-saxon world (and everywhere to a large degree) has followed a distinct pattern since World War Two. In the immediate post-war period Sorel was written about by fairly isolated and politically naïve academics who merely wished to produce a 'monograph' fitting somewhere within the prevailing concern to explain European fascism as the result of an irrational social impulse alien to the western democratic tradition. This was the 'strange tactics of extremism' period when ideology was ending and analysis in the universities took a holiday from political explicitness. Towards the end of the 1950s, the storm of reaction abated somewhat and more ambitious analyses appeared, which carried the search for the irrational roots of fascist authoritarianism to higher metaphysical levels. The re-publication of the English translation of Sorel's *Reflections on Violence* in 1951, with its consistent translation of 'class struggle' as 'class war', and one of its essays with references to Nietszche and epic heroism encouraged a view of Sorel as a traditional moralist of the nineteenth century, rather than as a marxist revolutionary. Before World War Two, however, Sorel was generally considered (as he is beginning to be considered

13

again), as an independent intellectual who made important contributions to what we call marxism.

It has only been since the emergence of a new revolutionary Left in the western world – since the social and political turbulence of the late 1960s and early 70s – that marxists and others began to study the works of Sorel seriously once again. In France this new attention has already produced some works which may very well 'rehabilitate' Sorel to a certain degree. Most notable is the chapter on Sorel in Daniel Lindenberg's *Le Marxisme introuvable* (Paris 1975), which attempts to describe 'the implantation of marxism in France'. A major part of Lindenberg's task was to reveal the importance of Sorel, whom he calls 'the isolated prophet of a proletarian marxism freed from the dead weight of positivist thinking'.[7] But it was Jacques Julliard, in a study of Sorel's personal and ideological comrade, Fernand Pelloutier, who broke the ground. Julliard's book, *Fernand Pelloutier et les origines du syndicalisme d'action directe* (Paris 1971), shows concretely how the combination of Pelloutier's syndicalist practice and the counsel of Sorel's analysis produced a 'true renaissance of marxism' in France during the mid-1890s – a renaissance which was stiffly opposed by both the orthodox school presided over by Jules Guesde, and the reformist branch of French socialism represented by Jean Jaurès.[8]

In 1977 the first major book on Sorel in thirty years appeared, Michel Charzat's *Georges Sorel et la révolution au XX^c siècle* (Paris 1977). It is a book which reveals nothing new and which is not particularly concerned to make a political point. But it is a major study which treats Sorel with the seriousness necessary, without the major distortions which characterise anglo-saxon writing on Sorel during the last thirty years. However, the new concern has extended to the English-speaking world as well.[9] In short, after decades of neglect coupled with frequent abuse, the written work of Georges Sorel is being considered seriously as a contribution to marxist social analysis.

Regardless of the new interest in Sorel, charges have been made against him that should be discussed. It has often been stated, for example, that Sorel's thinking went through a series of stages during which his political ideas changed radically. The implication is that he was ideologically unstable due to an alleged

14

lack of contact with the socialist movement, and that he was, thus, vulnerable to changes in intellectual fashion. This characterisation is false. Sorel did not change his socio-political perspective in a radical way at any time, and his contact with the socialist and proletarian movement was considerable. Most misconceptions regarding Sorel have emerged as the result of uninformed academic scholarship and the fact that, not having belonged to a political party or group, Sorel received no institutional or organised defence.

A common fallacy has been to separate real or imagined influences out of Sorel's overall concerns and to construct qualitative phases of development out of them. For example, Professor Michael Curtis has articulated the common variety of this kind of analysis by stating that Sorel was 'in turn a traditionalist in 1889, a marxist in 1894, a Bergsonian in the same year, a reformist syndicalist in 1904 to 1905, a disillusioned ex-Dreyfusard in 1909, an ally of the nationalists and monarchists in 1910, and at the time of World War One, a philosopher of morals'.[10] This is perhaps an extreme example of academic superficiality, but it illustrates well how failing to see the existence of ideas and the reality of politics in terms of a logical process can lead to analytical confusion.

More seriously, Sorel has been accused of fascist tendencies because of his stress upon the ideological dimension of political motivation, and because of his open discussion of the role of violence in social struggle. Professor Jack Roth has concluded, for example, that 'Fascism was indebted to Sorelismo', even though in 'nationalist and in some Fascist quarters there was outright hostility to Sorel – he was identified as the proponent of proletarian syndicalism and the defender of Lenin'.[11] Roth's article turns on a certain interpretation of Sorel's ideas, particularly the notion of 'myth' and the alleged 'irrationalist' context of Sorel's thought. His reasoning is that if Sorel was irrationalist and if fascism was irrationalist, then Sorel must have lent something to fascism, especially if some fascists could be found to have said they had read his books. In fact, Roth's most telling evidence against Sorel tends to maintain his innocence. 'By March 1922', Roth explains, Sorel 'stated that: "the two capital facts of the post-war era are: the action of Lenin, which I believe lasting, and

15

that of Mussolini, who will certainly triumph".'[12] Using Roth's reasoning we would have to call the MIR in Chile fascist for predicting a fascist *coup d'état* if Allende failed to arm the workers!

But the effect of such shabby exercises in logic has been considerable. Herbert Marcuse, for example, who generally has a more profound capacity for analysis has accepted such conclusions uncritically. 'Direct lines of development', he has said approvingly, 'have been drawn from Sorel's concept of social elites to both the proletarian "avant-garde" of leninism and to the elite "leaders" of fascism.'[13] Even Jean-Paul Sartre, discussing Frantz Fanon in his introduction to *The Wretched of the Earth*, refers to 'Sorel's fascist utterances'.[14] Can there be no fire where there is so much smoke?

In 1910 a book review written by Sorel appeared in the newspaper *Action Française*, the organ of a small group which would eventually emerge as France's leading fascist organisation during the 1920s and 30s. Sorel's review, a critique of a book written by Charles Peguy, was written for an Italian newspaper and was given to the *Action Française* without Sorel's knowledge. However, the fact that the review appeared in this reactionary context has led to the idea that Sorel embraced the ideas of the nationalist right. And Sorel himself encouraged the impression by agreeing to contribute to a literary journal animated by youthful aesthetes who turned out to be political reactionaries. When Sorel descovered the political orientation of his collaborators (who had solicited his participation), he refused to have anything more to do with them, but the damage had been done. The two incidents detract nothing from the value of Sorel's work, but they leave him open to criticism, in as much as his judgement failed him on at least the latter of the two occasions. If Sorel's lack of party connection allowed his analysis a certain freedom, it also presented a problem both personal and political in nature.

Sorel has been called a 'wild marxist', and there is a certain truth in the characterisation when we consider that he was not tamed by adherence to a political party or to a rigid frame of analytical reference, beyond his acceptance of historical materialism. In the western capitalist world we are used to thinking in terms of political parties – the key element of capitalist political democracy. And since the Bolshevik seizure of power in 1917, the party has also been the dominant model of revolutionary organisation. So we necessarily use the party as the touchstone of political evaluation, to the point where it has become difficult to imagine a revolutionary intellectual without the support and natural readership provided by affiliation with a political party.

In fact, Sorel did openly ally himself with a specific segment of the revolutionary movement – revolutionary syndicalism. He considered himself to be a spokesman for what he felt to be the proper attitude and strategy of revolutionaries everywhere. Yet he did this as an informed individual and not as the spokesman of a political tendency embodied in a political party. Had Sorel been a younger man when he began his involvement in the revolutionary movement, it is possible that he would have taken a more active role, at least to the extent of more frequent lecturing and agitating. However, it cannot be said that Sorel was isolated from the working-class movement or from revolutionary politics. During the last thirty years of his life he was a well-known figure on the revolutionary left in France.

His personal friends reflected his situation. Fernand Pelloutier, leading spirit in the founding of the *Bourses du Travail*, was the confidante who, in political terms at least, rated highest with him. It was Sorel who called upon the reformist Jean Jaurès, a man he did not particularly respect, to use his influence to obtain assistance from the state in order to sustain the dying Pelloutier.[15] Sorel's closest friend was Paul Delesalle, a respected worker militant, active in the General Confederation of Labour, who himself produced some effective articles and pamphlets on syndicalist strategy.

The question of the social foundations of Sorel's situation as a revolutionary intellectual is an important one, not only because of the misinterpretations that have arisen so frequently concerning it, but because no one who purports to speak in the interest of social emancipation can deny or expect to have his or her class background ignored. Sorel was not an 'organic intellectual' of the working class in the terms of Gramsci's conception; he did not emerge from the proletariat with an integral proletarian perspective. While Sorel's friend Paul Delesalle was such an 'organically' produced intellectual of the proletariat,

17

Sorel's class situation was more akin to that of Marx, Engels and Lenin. Sorel was alienated culturally and politically from his social class and lost his organic attachment to it. The conceptual break represented by his acceptance of marxist historical materialism, plus his rejection of what can be loosely termed as a 'bourgeois' lifestyle, meant that his relation to the revolutionary movement was more than one of mere verbal commitment.

Aware of his social origins and former status as a state functionary, Sorel consciously eliminated contradictions between his ideas and his daily life. One might contrast his efforts with those of Jaurès, who, although of working-class origins, attended France's most elite school (the *École normale supérieure*), had his children raised as good Catholics, and, as even his most supportive biographer admits, had a decided taste for the comforts of bourgeois life.[16] It is not necessary to romanticise poverty and the spartan lifestyle of revolutionary commitment, but revolutionary sentiments and ideals can be articulated more convincingly if they do not contradict the actual tastes and behaviour of the speaker. If a 'wild marxist', Sorel was also a rational and honest marxist during the thirty years he attempted to clarify the course of proletarian struggle.

In the following chapters I will discuss the marxism of Sorel in terms of its intellectual content and its practical application to the outstanding problems faced by the socialist and proletarian movements in France before World War One. Sorel's intellectual orientation (discussed in chapter two) is a question which involves a search for the philosophical roots of marxism and of what came to be the social sciences in general. His application of marxist analysis to practical political problems (the subject of chapter three) not only elucidates the inherently political nature of questions of marxist philosophy, but it illustrates how the controversy over 'revisionism' during the period of the Second Socialist International was a natural outgrowth of the general socialist movement. Chapters four and five discuss, respectively, 'revolutionary syndicalism' – considered by Sorel to be the most legitimate strategy for proletarian revolution, and the problem of 'embourgeoisement' – the spread of bourgeois ideology to the working class, a phenomenon that he considered to be the greatest threat to the revolutionary movement.

18

2. Marxism and Bourgeois Sociology: The Analytical Poles of Class Conflict

Sorel's intellectual formation as a marxist was unique in that he neither emerged from the working class as a socialist intellectual with first hand proletarian experience, nor did he become radicalised as a student in an academic milieu. Because he was exposed to marxism during his full intellectual maturity and when most of his personal, existential problems were resolved the emotional content of his commitment did not lead him into dogma. He attempted to discover the real scientific foundations of marxism in the logic of its orientation to socio-historical phenomena. It was an effort that naturally involved a consideration of what is now called the philosophy of social science.

Before the existence of effective, large scale working-class organisation and strike action in France, there was no social science in that country. The connection is simple, causal and is not negated at all by efforts to trace the emergence of the central ideas and methods of this social science over a long period of time. Before the 1890s in France, bourgeois ideology was informed by a view of social reality which shared some essential elements with marxism itself. Of primary importance was a view of social classes which assumed automatically that almost unbridgeable cultural divisions maintained social distance between them. One has only to read Émile Zola to understand how even the latest thinking on genetics could reinforce this social perspective. Throughout most of the second half of the nineteenth century this view of the social world prevailed in France, and it was articulated most scientifically by the Frédéric LePlay school of social analysis, which is discussed here because it illustrates how the French ruling classes were to radically alter their view of socio-political reality towards the end of the century.

LePlay's view was formed during the Second Empire phase of political reaction following the suppression of the working

19

classes during the aftermath of the 1848 revolution and Louis Bonaparte's coup d'état. LePlay's work consisted of detailed investigations of working-class life which were designed to provide guidelines for what was then considered social reform. Lacking most of the more modern statistical techniques and concern for 'value-free' analysis which characterises contemporary sociology, this social analysis involved an unselfconscious projection of an almost pre-industrial world view. While there was concern about new phenomena such as rapid urbanisation and industrialisation, society was still explained in terms of the same cultural relations between social classes which had prevailed since before the French Revolution. The working class was considered passive by nature and could be aroused, for good or ill, only by its betters, who were called forthrightly, the 'social authorities' or the 'patrons'. If workers tried to effect their own destiny by forming defence committees or by striking, the responsibility ultimately lay with the social authorities, the bosses, priests and political officials who had the natural duty to inform and direct the 'lower classes', who were considered lower in every sense – even to the extent of their intelligence quotient. Consequently, even though the 1870s and 80s saw a gradual renewal of working-class organisation, supporters of the social status quo had no profound fears regarding its stability.

Methodologically this 'pre-sociology' relied upon field investigation exploring the nature of family life among the workers and their customs in general. The techniques of LePlay and his followers were basically those which are today associated with cultural anthropologists. And, in fact, the working classes were thought of at this time as a sort of aboriginal population – primitive, essentially lethargic, but impressionable, and for that reason at least it was important to understand them thoroughly so as to defend them against bad influences. The ideological dimension of this approach to the study of society was clear and no attempt was made to hide it: the working classes must be encouraged to accept social relations as they exist through the example set by the social authorities and by the intelligent exercise of paternalistic control. There should be no equal 'dealing' with the workers, but rather a 'demonstration' of how they should conduct themselves. This was a social perspective which conformed perfectly to the semi-spiritual 'moralism' which characterised the philosophy of the time; it placed a high priority on cultural values – ethical, juridical and familial. This was the state of 'sociology' throughout Sorel's early life and it was still the dominant mind-set when he settled in Paris in 1892.

Sorel's timing was good because it was just then that a series of events was shattering the old view represented by LePlayist social philosophy. Beginning dramatically on May Day 1891, a three year period opened during which French society appeared to be coming apart at its seams. On May Day, all of France was shocked by the unprovoked shooting of a number of demonstrating workers. The effect on public opinion was similar to that provoked by the Kent State shooting in the United States in 1970. It appeared that constituted authority had lost its guiding intelligence and that opposing factions within it had lost any basis for rational communication. Strike activity quickly mounted to unprecedented levels. Socialists entered on electoral lists scored unheard-of successes in 1892 and 1893. In July of 1893 there was more than a week of student riots in Paris which at least once spilled over to merge with workers engaged in their own struggles with the state and the bosses. And, if this was not enough, these years were the very time that anarchist 'propaganda by the deed' was carving out its well-known niche in history. The names Vailliant, Henry and Ravachol soon caused shivers to run up bourgeois spines as police stations, judges' residences, public buildings, the Chamber of Deputies, and even restaurants and cafes began to explode in rapid succession. Class against class rhetoric was everywhere in the air, and the tactics of modern revolutionary 'agit-prop' achieved near contemporary sophistication. For revolutionaries of all tendencies, the first five years of the 1890s were a time when action inspired action at a breath-taking pace and the only limits placed on the possibilities for social transformation seemed to result from a lack of experience. It was true that the anarchist actions, culminating in the assassination of the President of the Republic in June 1894, facilitated the passage of the repressive *lois scélérates* which gave the police free reign to intimidate revolutionaries on an individual basis, but even this could not dampen the developing optimism. Socialists, therefore, were naturally concerned with

21

the forward thrust of their movement and not fully cognisant of reaction to it among the established powers; this reaction, while not having the immediate effect of expanded police powers, would come to exert a major brake on the revolutionary struggle. The emergence of 'bourgeois sociology' as a theoretical inspiration and justification for new methods of counter-revolution began immediately upon the rise of the revolutionary movement, but only Sorel and a few others recognised its importance at the time.

The unprecedented combination of events in the early 1890s in France was perceived as a sort of fundamental breakdown, a disintegration of basic social bonds. As such, the perception cut the ground from under the old LePlayist view of 'natural', paternalistic relations between the classes, and it made ridiculous the '*laissez faire*' conception of government's role in socio-economic affairs. Progressive bourgeois thought was returning towards the idea that the state would be obliged to play an increasingly important role not only in industrial struggles, but in the very formation of social attitudes. The emergence of modern sociology in France was a direct result of these revelations. The outstanding early proponents – Gabriel Tarde, Gustave LeBon, and Émile Durkheim – were primarily concerned to locate the psychological dynamic behind the manifestations of social disintegration and to indicate ways in which the alienation causing it could be eliminated in the interest of social order. Durkheim especially would come to bring an intricately built support to the changing direction of state politics, in the form of a modern research group enjoying firm ties with the political establishment, active intervention in questions of social policy, and a profound modification of both the techniques and content of education at virtually every level. The emergence of sociology was thus part of a general structural response of the capitalist polity to the threat posed by a sudden surge of the working-class movement.

Sorel gave special consideration to the rise of a French 'sociology' at a time when other socialists were attempting to cope with what seemed to be more concrete problems. As mentioned previously, Sorel even attended Durkheim's defence of his doctoral thesis (published in English as *The Division of*

Labour in Society) and his growing acquaintance with the French academic world during the years 1892-95 gave him a profound and unusually acute perspective on the subtle changes of attitude and thinking among the ruling classes. Sorel was not a young student, with an unformed, easily impressionable mind, but a mature and intelligent engineer turned towards social philosophy on a practical basis. With a scientifically-trained eye he examined the subterranean academic movement which would eventually surface as an ideological and political counter-attack on the proletariat. It was in developing his critique of the new sociology that Sorel was first able to supplement the marxism of his time with a more nuanced conception of social alienation, a theme which only lately has emerged as a major focus of attention for marxists.

In 1893, Sorel published three review articles dealing with the work of Cesare Lombroso, the leading representative of the Italian school of 'criminal anthropology', the ideas of which concerning lower-class behaviour reflected those of the bourgeoisie at the time. Lombroso was attempting to lend scientific foundation to the simplistic (and rather nineteenth century 'naturalistic') notion of the 'born criminal' which conveniently assumed that crime was the manifestation of some hereditary defect in the individual, and not the result of social conditioning. Once again, even people sympathetic to the condition of working people, like Émile Zola, were frequently under the spell of such ideas. In rejecting this vulgar evolutionism, which supported the elitist thinking of the bourgeoisie, Sorel argued that crime could be considered more legitimately as conscious or unconscious acts of rebellion against civic authority.[1] But the important distinction to make was that such behavioural phenomena had to be considered from the standpoint of the influence of the social milieu, not from that of biology. On the other hand, Sorel could agree with Lombroso that most parliamentary legislation could be thought of as a conscious attempt to forestall alienation from political society,[2] but the facts pointed to a certain contradiction within Lombroso's thinking: the comfortable thought that crime is the result of a 'low-born' character did not fit in perfectly with the practical realisation that the state could modify behaviour through its structuring of the socio-cultural environment.

23

It was through his critique of ideas like those of Lombroso that Sorel came to realise the significance of an important formulation of Durkheim's which came to light clearly in the latter's *Suicide*. Durkheim demonstrated that different modes of human behaviour can have the same social motives. The realisation that crime in general, suicide, prostitution and other forms of what the sociologists considered 'abnormal' behaviour, could have the same social roots, was, from a marxist perspective, an important step towards a developed conception of socio-cultural alienation.[3]

Sorel perceived that Lombroso and the rest of the Italian school were having an important impact on the new sociology; but he soon discovered that sociology in France was much more advanced. When he turned his attention to the ideas of Durkheim, Le Bon and Tarde he discovered more important considerations. For, in spite of his dislike of the political implications of Durkheim's work, Sorel recognised its scientific potential. Rather than simply translating the reigning social morality into pseudo-theoretical terms, Durkheim was genuinely attempting to express a detached 'scientific' consideration of events and phenomena in logical, relatively value-free terms.

Sorel saw quickly that the scientific 'objectivity' then being proclaimed by marxists had found its equivalent in Durkheim's conception of the scientific 'normality' of the 'social fact'. Even Gabriel Tarde, whose work represented a major conceptual advance over that of the LePlayist school, still approached the study of society from the standpoint of a traditional moralist. Tarde, according to Sorel, believed that 'the norm is peace in justice and light, it is the complete extermination of crime, of vice, of ignorance, misery and abuse'. Thus, whatever innovations Tarde may have produced in the field of sociology, he was 'still stuck in the naïve optimism of the eighteenth century. He believes in the innate goodness of humanity and the cure of all human evils with good will.' Durkheim on the other hand, was much more realistic. Sorel agreed with him that 'in all research it is necessary to understand that we are concerned with given forces, in the light of specific conditions. Before announcing the end of poverty and crime, it is necessary to know if poverty and crime do not depend upon psycho-physiological and economic

24

factors over which we have no immediate control.'[4] Only working within these general analytical outlines could sociologists hope to be scientific.

It must not be thought, however, that Sorel believed Durkheim to have actually arrived at a truly 'objective' approach to the study of social phenomena. Durkheim's conception of the 'normal' retained normative values which harked back to the old moral philosophy. The difference was that Durkheim was now stressing the primacy of the social over the moral (in general discourse if not in strict epistemological terms), and this indicated a turning towards a more realistic understanding of social processes.

Sorel reaffirmed his belief in the importance of the new sociology by devoting the lead article of the first number of *Le Devenir social* to a critical analysis of Durkheim's recently published *The Rules of Sociological Method* (1895). Durkheim, in Sorel's estimation, would clearly come nearer to 'science' in the practice of sociology than most other aspirants in the field if he were to follow the methodological principles set forth in the book. He had established his method before his investigations began and he self-consciously maintained a rigorous conceptual framework. Furthermore, he seemed to have come closer to solving the principal problem of social science: the dichotomy between 'fact' and 'value'. Sorel was most impressed to read in Durkheim that a study of society is not limited to a knowledge of one or more 'empirical relations', because although each empirically demon-strated relationship involves a strong causal presumption, it is necessary to examine each in relation to the others.[5] In the final analysis, Durkheim's big contribution was to go beyond a descriptive approach to the study of social phenomena. In contrast to the LePlayists, who believed themselves to be entirely objective while exhibiting the most unsubtle biases, Durkheim employed a systematised analytical framework which recognised the necessity of prior assumptions about the data, but which was designed to minimise distorted conclusions by being rigorously consistent in analysis.[6] Sorel admired this approach for the conceptual rigour it demanded, and because it approximated to the techniques he found inherent in marxist sociology. Thus, for Sorel, 'objectivity' in social analysis resulted from a combination

25

of systematic method and a consciously formulated philosophical orientation. All phenomenological conclusions should be consistent with observed reality and rendered communicable through the use of an analogical terminology adopted for the purpose. But it was important that the analogues used should bear some meaningful relation to the society itself, a factor which ruled out the nineteenth-century use of biological imagery which dominated social conceptualisation in France, including that of Durkheim.

In criticising Durkheim's work, Sorel was able to expose certain problems related to the use of analogy in social conceptualism, especially its ideological implications. Besides the well-known organismic theory of social process with its elaborate metaphors of specialised function – hygiene, sickness, amputation, brain, nervous system, and so on – Sorel discussed other systems of analogy which were just as applicable. Meteorology, for example, could provide a terminology illuminative of social dynamics. The concept of 'frequency' was necessary in dealing with the incidence and recurrence of phenomena, as was the concept of a 'central nucleus' which could be used to explain governmental administration, a system of irrigation or storm centres in roughly the same terms. The problem with any such system of analogical language is that its use quickly passes beyond a conceptual heuristic, and becomes an imaginitive substitute for the reality it is supposed to portray. The use of biological terminology had, for example, become so convoluted that it rendered social processes almost devoid of sense. Sorel never tired of pointing out that the biological science of his day had borrowed many of its central conceptions from early studies of society like Malthus' work on population. He went so far as to say that 'the expressions employed in biology are almost all borrowed from sociology'. Thus, to use biological language in social conceptualisation was to use a thirdhand terminology.[7] While, up to a certain point, analogical language clarifies meaning, it soon intervenes to eliminate it. (His cautioning might easily be extended to include the marxist 'infrastructure-superstructure' dichotomy, in as much as it can lead to a simplistic determinism.)

Sorel raised another such question in his critique of Durkheim's work concerning the notion of 'milieu', the qualitative environment surrounding or producing an event. He was very wary of this expression, since by its very nature a 'milieu' cannot be empirically defined. He noted that the notion of 'system', while more limited than that of 'milieu' might be used to better advantage. In a sense, then, a 'milieu' could be reduced to a system by a delineation of the set of relations surrounding the object of study. Thus, while the use of analogical terminology was dangerous there was really no way of discarding it entirely; after all is considered, the object of social analysis is communication.

Far from wishing to eliminate analogical abstractions from social conceptualisation, Sorel advocated the replacement of organismic or geological analogues with those from the domain of physics, which he believed to be more appropriate to the actual functioning of industrial-capitalist society. Force, friction, mass, momentum, acceleration, movement in general, these were some of the terms which Sorel felt were most apt in describing modern social dynamics. With respect to the problem of describing or defining a milieu, for example, Sorel explained that it could legitimately be considered as a sort of 'force field' where repellent or attractive agents exist in a state of mutual tension. He considered this conception more amenable to a materialistic consideration of politics and society. In the end, his preoccupation with the 'relational' situation of phenomena involved a consideration of environmental dialectics.

But the goal of social analysis should not be merely to describe social reality in static terms, no matter how much attention is given to the 'dialectical method'. The conception of 'milieu', for example, should involve a consideration of movement both in time and through time; and it was here that Sorel found the new sociology to be on a very weak footing. While Durkheim had written his entire doctoral thesis on the division of labour in society, he neglected the movement of the social groups formed by the division of labour. For this reason above all others marxism would seem to be much closer to being a science than would bourgeois sociology.

> Socialism introduces . . . a factor systematically neglected by the sociologists, it does not at all separate the division of

27

labour and the formation of classes. The latter, organised for struggle, exert an important influence on the division of labour by introducing some forces very different from those discussed by Durkheim. Thanks to the conception of class struggle we can follow the real historical process, while Durkheim's approach is simply schematic and logical.

Thanks to the theory of classes, socialists do not refer to the objectives of imaginary entities, to the needs of the collective spirit and other sociological claptrap, but rather to real people formed in groups acting in social life. It is thus that socialists have opened a new way to psychological research and permitted it to take a great part in sociological investigation. They mark the directions into which [sociology] must push its analyses.[8]

But if marxist socialists were breaking new ground in the field of social analysis and thus marking the direction that sociology must take, the political uses of the new concerns and techniques would be very different from what socialist revolutionaries would like to see. The increase of social knowledge produced by the working-class and socialist movements would be used by the sociologists to retard those movements, and Sorel warned socialists to be aware of the political potential of the new sociology:

Socialism has found an adversary of the first order. Durkheim . . . is for the organisation and intervention of the state and he approaches these problems in a very progressive spirit. The new ideas on conservative democracy, assuring more justice in economic relations, favouring the intellectual and moral formation of the people, and pushing industry along more scientific paths, have finally found a theoretician who is, at the same time, a metaphysician of rare subtlety and a scholar perfectly armed for the struggle.[9]

The following decades bore out Sorel's observation more than he could have imagined. Durkheimian sociology proved to be an important bulwark of capitalist ideology not only in France but throughout the entire western world. It is unfortunate that marxists did not keep abreast of the very techniques they inspired. Failing to expose the ideological content of academic sociology allowed a formidable counter-revolutionary force to develop, *without* the development of what came to be called 'critical theory' some decades later.

At a time when marxist socialism still carried a lot of utopian baggage from the nineteenth century which was manifested in a rigid adherence to a simplistic expectation of how the revolutionary struggle would unfold, Sorel attempted to clarify the relation between theory and practice in a way which admitted the complexity of the problem. Even before his exploration of marxist dialectics, Sorel publicly expressed the importance of maintaining a working relationship between theory and practice. In a critique of prevailing assumptions underlying the study of physics which he published in 1892, he pointed out that 'atomism' and determinism in general involved a confusion of 'physical representations' with 'hypotheses'. From an epistemological point of view, Sorel insisted that 'a representation is purely logical and is not at all capable of explaining knowledge. It is part of written and spoken language' but it is a tool and nothing more.[10]

Sorel himself advocated an approach lying somewhere between empiricism and idealism (what today would be called a materialist phenomenology) and a dynamic as opposed to a static conception of physical reality. Consideration of the effects of time, duration, perception and deformed consciousness were absolutely necessary for all scientists, physical, social or otherwise. All analysts must be open and subtle enough to cope with the 'successive effects of shocks and the fusions of rapidly succeeding sensations'. 'Everyone knows', Sorel explained, 'that a moving body with sufficient speed can give the illusion of a luminous line.' The point was that 'this phenomenon of fusion does not obey a simple arithmetical law; the sensation cannot be derived from the mean'.[11] Thus empiricist and determinist approaches to the analysis of phenomena cannot explain either their nature or their actions.

The key to Sorel's philosophical orientation (apart from its materialist first premises) was movement, both through time and between phenomena. Conditions such as force, friction, acceleration, speed and mass which had recently found their way into the teaching of relevant disciplines, meant that 'mankind is not at all condemned to error between empiricism and idealism'.[12] Conceptual breakthroughs and technological progress had brought a realisation that real physical processes and our knowledge of them are apprehended through a conception of dynamic, symbiotic relationships which could be called 'dialectical'. And, just as there can be no completely theoretical physics, there can be no valuable social philosophy which does not bear a direct relation to actual social processes.

In the absence of Marx's early writings, which have in more recent decades clarified his philosophical approach, especially *The Economic and Philosophical Manuscripts of 1844*, Sorel referred to other sources which served the same instructional function, if read within the proper context. Especially important was his reading of the German philosopher Franz Reuleaux, whose work focused upon the relationship between machines and human mentality. As Sorel would do later, Reuleaux denounced 'vulgar empiricism' and the 'increasing tendency to reduce questions about machines to simple problems of pure mechanics'.[13]

Reuleaux defined his object of study as 'cinematics'; it was the science of movement and the changes wrought by movement. Methodologically, Reuleaux's concern was to reconcile theory and practice, insisting that 'theory need not always march behind practice. It is on the footing of reciprocal value that theory and practice must be placed in relation to each other.'[14] The overall objective of this 'cinematics' was invention – the end product of imagination properly stimulated by the environment. 'Cinematic' synthesis does not diminish the intellectual work of the inventor – it raises it. 'It permits him to see more clearly the end he desires and the means at his disposal, at the same time he grasps the method to follow in order to utilise these means.'[15]

In addition to this practical approach to phenomenological considerations, Reuleaux offered Sorel some fairly penetrating insights about social and historical development, including a notion of alienated labour very similar to that of Marx. Reuleaux observed: 'today in certain cases machinery has reached such a degree of automaticity that it has begun to be almost completely substituted for people whose genius has invented and animated it and who require it to achieve their ends. Meanwhile, by a cruel irony, people began to feel lowered to the rank of machines.'[16] In addition Reuleaux offered certain conceptual heuristics that were as important as his substantive observations. In studying the transformations in work caused by machines he stated, there were 'two principal directions: the *form* of the movement, and the *force* of it'. And force itself must be qualified as 'apparent force' or 'latent force'.[17]

Sorel would ultimately apply these conceptions to the questions of revolutionary strategy posed by the working-class movement and the class struggle. For example, the concepts of apparent and latent force were relevant to his later consideration of social violence. More specifically, the very idea of revolutionary class consciousness involves the assumption that there is a potential or 'latent' force immanent in proletarian psychology. Yet the importance that Sorel placed on the fusion of theory and practice kept him from accepting the idealist mysteries which characterised the thinking of people such as Freud and Bergson. Because he believed that thought could not be explained outside of its relation to the social environment, Sorel could discuss quality with direct reference to quantity and deal with process in abstract terms without recourse to teleology. As an engineer, Sorel abhorred abstraction *in vacuo* and this horror accounts for his frequent attacks upon 'rationalism' – thinking which is predicated only upon thought itself in the crypto-idealist and positivistic way which predominated in the France of his time. It was this same 'rationalist' positivism which Lenin exposed as bourgeois ideology in his *Materialism and Empirio-Criticism* (1910). Sorel felt that social analysts should be actively engaged in the reality they were examining, they should apply their ideas and gain the concrete understanding which allows a grasp of dynamic processes. In sum, he advocated a mode of thought founded upon a unity of theory and practice, and anti-'intellectualist' and anti-'rationalist' in its aversion to idealist speculations.

Sorel's thought was formed by a combination of certain intellectual influences and by the work process itself. A well-trained engineer is necessarily pragmatic and realistic while

31

combining a close attention to detail with a capacity for analytical extrapolation. Above all, Sorel's work required a unitary conception of planning and application – 'theory' and 'practice'. In fact, an engineer must *not* think in terms of two categories – theory *and* practice – but must rather consider his or her work as a total process involving both mental and physical work, and a consideration of detail within the context of a vision, a prior conception, of the completed work. For an engineer, therefore, it would be absurd to categorise his or her work as involving an 'empiricist' perspective, or an 'idealist', or even a materialist one. Thus Sorel's philosophical orientation was not merely a product of his reading, but also of the work process (something which generally applies to everyone). To say that Sorel's thought was the result of his reading of the prominent authors of his time, merely because he wrote about them, fails to penetrate beyond the topical content of a written work and, thus, fails to recognise how thought is only part of a practical process.[18]

Yet there is the question of the 'content' of Sorel's thought, especially in relation to his approach to marxism. If the ideas of Franz Reuleaux lent themselves to Sorel's intellectual habits and to his general approach to phenomenological process, it was the work of the French socialist Pierre-Joseph Proudhon which added formative content to his social and political vision.

Proudhon's work lent itself to Sorel's initiation into what he would eventually recognise as historical materialism; for, regardless of the fact that Proudhon was an idealist, his work was rich with social and political analysis of the class structure and the problems facing the working-class movement. In spite of Marx's generally correct polemic against Proudhon in *The Poverty of Philosophy*, there are many similarities in Marx's and Proudhon's views of capitalist society. For Sorel, it was clearly Proudhon's discussion of class consciousness that influenced him most and which contributed to his relatively advanced understanding of the importance of ideology in the class struggle.

For Proudhon, the content of class consciousness in a specific period essentially determines the form political activity will assume. Proudhon's best formulation of this perspective is found in his *The Political Capacity of the Working Classes* (1865), a work which Sorel knew extremely well and to which he referred often. Proudhon observed that, while class relations may change in important ways, changes in socio-political consciousness do not necessarily change with them; and the key was to be found in the *culture* of the working classes in relation to that of the ruling classes.

> From the origins of society the plebeian worker has lived dependently upon the possessing class, and consequently in a mental state of profound intellectual and moral inferiority. It has only been since yesterday, since the revolution of 1789 broke the social hierarchy, that this feeling of inferiority has become an element of proletarian self-consciousness. Nevertheless the impulse towards social deference is still powerful . . . Those who were formerly masters and who have retained the privileges of the so-called 'liberal' professions continue to seem a foot taller than others. Add to this the jealousy that the working people direct against their peers who aspire to rise above their 'condition' and you cannot be surprised when, after already having been forced to adapt to new social conditions and new ideologies, the People have retained their habitual abnegation.[19]

Thus Proudhon focused upon the problem of political consciousness in relation to social transformation and the maintenance of the cultural dominance of the ruling class from the standpoint of his consideration of working-class psychology. As long as the working class respected ruling-class culture enough to feel inferior in relation to it, they would lack a revolutionary perspective and thus the capacity to overthrow the bourgeoisie and forge new social relations. For Proudhon, the problem was posed by the seeming incapacity of the working classes to take advantage of the opportunity to advance their interests by the vote (in the plebiscites of the Second Empire workers consistently voted directly against their own best interests).

Proudhon concluded that the political capacity of the working class should be considered both in terms of its 'legal' capacity and its 'real' capacity. The task of revolutionaries was generally one of encouraging the working class to realise its 'real' capacity – its potential political capacity – and thus to

33

be able to take advantage of its 'legal' capacity (or 'opportunities'). A number of conditions would be required to achieve 'real' capacity: firstly that workers be conscious of themselves, their dignity and value in society; secondly that as a result of this consciousness the workers form an abstract idea of themselves which incorporates this value and *raison d'être*; and thirdly that the abstract idea, articulated as a conviction, leads to practical courses of action in accordance with 'need and the diversity of circumstances'. Put in more concrete terms, the working class must first 'distinguish itself from the bourgeoisie', form an abstract and positive image of its own class, and then take action designed to eliminate the injustices which have existed because of the class system. Proudhon believed that the working class had fulfilled the first two criteria, but that it was far from being capable of carrying out class conscious political action. He felt that the government was doing much to keep the workers from developing a clearer class vision.

Sorel's reading of Proudhon obviously merged with his subsequent understanding of the more complete and philosophically well-founded works of Marx. It would be a simple matter for Sorel to translate Proudhon's idea of real political capacity into a marxist conception of revolutionary class consciousness. The element of potentiality found in the notions of 'latent political capacity' and in the 'realisation' of revolutionary class consciousness represents a shared dynamic element which, when joined with Franz Reuleaux's categories of 'apparent' and 'latent force', does much to clarify the sources of Sorel's approach to marxist analysis. On a more abstract level, it is equally important that the fundamental hegelian conception of 'being in a state of becoming' was a philosophical affinity which bound together the thinking of Proudhon, Marx and Sorel – one which distinguished their thinking sharply from the kantianism and positivism which dominated bourgeois philosophy then, and now.

By 1897 Sorel's greater familiarity with Marx's work confirmed his initial impression that the ideas of the latter were not properly understood, despite Marx's prominence in the European socialist movement. Part of the problem was merely a lack of adequate translation, but the major obstacle was the attitude of French socialists who, out of ignorance or commitment to certain political interests, misrepresented Marx's work. 'Marxism', Sorel wrote to Benedetto Croce, 'is far from being the doctrine and method of Marx. In the hands of disciples devoid of sufficient historical knowledge and philosophical criticism, marxism has become a caricature. "Return to Marx", that is my motto and I believe it is the best way.'[20] Objecting particularly to the vulgarisation of marxist analysis represented by economic determinism (or 'economic materialism' as it was sometimes called at the time), Sorel said in his preface to Antonio Labriola's *Socialism and Philosophy*: 'some people insist that, according to Marx, all political, moral and aesthetic phenomena are determined . . . but Marx is not responsible for this caricature of his historical materialism.'[21]

At the very least, Sorel was a marxist who can in no way be cast into the category which contemporary observers call 'classical marxism'. His grasp of dialectical process in general and the dynamics of ideological formation in particular were as subtle as necessary without falling into the philosophical formalism which afflicts much of contemporary marxism. Sorel's writings are many and they range widely, making it difficult to cull a 'theory' from them. But this is as it should be, because a real marxist uses his or her pen to expose and attack capitalism and the enemies of socialism more directly than those who are concerned only to advance themselves by pretending to advance 'marxism' on a metaphysical level. Rather than present some sort of textual synthesis, I can present Sorel's essential understanding of marxism in the form of his own spontaneous presentation, when he defended marxism against criticism from the bourgeois academic establishment.

On 20 March 1902 Sorel presented a paper on the subject of historical materialism to the French Philosophical Society, of which he was a member.[22] He began his presentation by explaining the problems connected with a systematic discussion of historical materialism, pointing out that neither Marx nor Engels had directly outlined the precepts and method of the materialist conception of history, and that it is difficult to abstract these operative principles from the individual works since none does justice to the complexity of the entire system. He added that the

35

difficulty is inevitably encountered when dealing with a philosophy which, at base, attempts to synthesise theory and action. He made reference to Croce in saying that historical materialism is not a given formula nor a mere philosophy of history, nor just a method, but rather 'a sum of new givens, of new experiences which have entered into the consciousness of the historian'. Like any 'theory founded in practice', he said, historical materialism 'is essentially a doctrine of prudence furnishing people with a means of understanding the dangers confronting them; it must teach us to distinguish what flows from liberty (what happens according to rational volition) from that which happens because of natural necessity.'

This was the most general conceptual and methodological thrust of historical materialism. More substantively, the conception was based upon a perception, shared by Marx and Hegel, that 'civil society' is a 'determined' environment, one defined by Sorel as the mode of social organisation in which needs are satisfied following a determinate division of economic functions and the administration and enforcement of justice. It is upon this 'base' that 'juridical, political, and philosophical structures' are raised. Political life results from the conflicts and reconciliations of the different social groups corresponding to the division of economic functions. These conflicts are motivated by the clash of differing, real 'interests', but they are expressed in terms of ideas and attitudes formalised in juridical law. Thus, ultimately, class interests are articulated (and ruling class interests are defended) by specific principles of justice. 'Borrowing from Hegel', Sorel stated, 'Marx considered people as characterised by a certain manner of obtaining their income. Each group forms juridical ideas conforming to its function, ideas which permeate all our thinking . . .' The political conflicts between these groups provide the focus for marxist historical and social analysis.

Sorel ended his lecture by an attempt to deal with the question of economic determinism and its relation to marxism; in doing so he articulated what Marx best expressed in his then unknown *The German Ideology* concerning the relationship between ideas and the social environment:

The juridical and political conceptions of man do not
36

necessarily correspond to their trade; they are also made up of freely acquired convictions which are preached as social doctrine.

Thus there was no *direct* correspondence between economic interests and political ideology, and therein lies the work of the individual revolutionaries – to help bring about a clear and generalised proletarian consciousness of how working-class interests require the elimination of capitalist productive and social relations. Far from being directed by unseen social and economic forces, men and women because of the existence of marxism, understand their condition to the point where they can exert their own will on it and thus effect historical development:

> The socialist conception is founded upon the possibility of creating a common spirit in the modern proletariat which, it is hoped, will lead the world into a state of liberty – to a state where reasoned will can realise its plans in a system of production that will have become profoundly scientific.

Historical materialism is, therefore, not a systematised philosophy, but rather an 'approach' to the study of social reality, based to be sure on certain philosophical premises, and involving an unavoidable commitment to change and transcendence of capitalist ideology and social relations.

Sorel's presentation was received with a certain amount of scepticism by the professors. Did not Marx say that ideals are determined by material factors? Isn't, 'according to Marx', Sorel was asked, 'action of the "spiritual" upon the "material", of the "theoretical" upon the "practical", an impossibility?' Isn't it true that people's reason can only reflect 'the material activity of a given time'? Sorel's assertion of the unity of theory and practice in Marx's thought was also challenged. Wasn't it true that Marx's ideas were only related to practice in that they represented an ideal, a utopian vision of a society in which economic injustices would be eliminated?

These responses were probably exactly what Sorel had expected from his audience. Even more than the majority of the marxists of the time, bourgeois academics remained rooted in the mechanical determinism of the nineteenth century. Economic determinism was the only way that most of these men could have possibly understood marxism, giving their education and general social class orientation.

Yet Sorel's attempt to clarify how determinism could be transcended by a dialectical consideration of socio-historical phenomena was an important enough event in the development of French marxism. On this occasion he explained that Marx's analyses and his philosophy were themselves rooted in historical processes, yet self-consciously so in a concerted attempt to effect those same historical processes; for this reason it is impossible to separate theory and practice in Marx's work. Marxists themselves must not elevate Marx's words above their historical context: like all other historical phenomena marxism must be approached historically, so that determinism and idealistic reifications do not result. The 'subjective' content of ideas – conscious or unconscious motives, goals, intentions – should be as seriously considered as the structural context. In no case should the observations of phenomena be made with the formulation of 'historical laws' as an objective. Marx, for example, was not interested in devising a theory: he had no university promotion or salary increase to worry about. He had rather a practical, disinterested goal: the formation of a revolutionary proletarian class consciousness.

To analyse social reality according to Marx's method, Sorel explained, one should focus upon the dynamic relation existing between social classes, political actions and ideology, especially ideology as manifested in juridical conceptions. Above all, socio-historical phenomena must be analysed in terms of the conflicting social interests resulting from the organisation of material production. Sorel emphasised that it is in Marx's 'particular manner of conceiving the division of society into classes' that the originality of his thought lies. The notion of historical class struggle enables one to go beyond both the 'great man' approach to history and the idea of fortuitous, directionless development. Because of the way in which social classes are formed, ideology can be construed as a mirror reflecting class interests and contradictions, however distorted – or, as a prism, since, as Sorel explained, conceptions of right and wrong do not necessarily reflect class interests directly.

38

The objective existence of competing social classes is, however, not a sufficient conditioning for the unfolding of revolutionary class struggle as envisaged by Marx. Although classes exist because of the social relations required by capitalist production, a class 'is characterised by a feeling of unity and national organisation' only 'when the class has attained its full maturity'. And although classes exist because of productive relations, class relationships are expressed through formal juridical codes, The 'division' of classes, going beyond the productive causes of their division, is only a reality when there is a sufficent degree of consciousness of the disparity of justice endemic to a particular society; and this rigorous division of ideas with respect to the law explains how it is possible to speak of classes as separate entities. 'The separation exists only in so far as the juridical consciousnesses of the classes are clearly separated . . .' The role of marxist analysis and socialist action must be to expose juridical disparities to the point where the mass of the proletariat clearly perceives a system of class justice and realises that social liberation depends upon the abolition of capitalist production and the formal and informal inequalities of human rewards caused by it. Before there can be a *conscious* movement of class there must be a movement of opinion; and this is why the primary work of those already in possession of revolutionary consciousness is the formulation and dissemination of propaganda.

All of Marx's intellectual work was both philosophical analysis and such propaganda. It was at once a scholarly analysis of social reality and an inspiration to the cause of socialist revolution. It was, therefore, founded upon and characterised by a synthesis of theory and action. Sorel went on to state that when he spoke 'of a union of theory and practice, I mean a union in the sense used in the so-called applied sciences'. Marx's work simply cannot be broken up into separate abstract components – theory and political propaganda – it is both. It is necessary to penetrate to essentials when studying Marx and marxism, and 'what is essential is the formation of class consciousness'.

Then, and now, this question of 'consciousness' was far from academic. And in recent years the question of ideological struggle has come to be considered the major problem for revolutionaries in the industrial-capitalist west. This dimension of revolutionary combat has always existed, but during the formative period of working-class organisation in France it was generally felt that the mere force of socio-economic contradictions within the rapidly evolving productive system would maintain clearcut class divisions. Thus, it seemed, a basic minimum of class consciousness could be taken for granted. This perhaps understandable complacency must be taken into account seriously whenever the 'determinism' of what is sometimes called 'classical' marxism is considered. Both the proletarian movement and socialist electoral politics were still in their very earliest years; and all the difficulty and complexity of revolutionary politics was not yet known.

When we look now at some of the major developments in social theory which emerged from this period of political experimentation, we understand how practical innovations tended to create illusions and then disillusionment. The socialist (and marxist) 'revisionism' of the late 1890s, which was best articulated by Eduard Bernstein, represented, on the immediate political level, a certain optimism about recent gains in socialist electoral efforts in relation to the regularity with which strikes turned into heroically fought failures. Revisionism also represented a growing realisation that the capitalist economy, and polity, had a capacity for continued growth and flexibility that most revolutionaries were reluctant to admit. It was quite reasonable, therefore, for the latest generation of socialists – who were generally not case-hardened by the struggles of earlier, more rigorous years – to turn towards a gradualist interpretation of capitalist development and towards electoral reformism as *the* road to socialism. By the time the optimism wore off, the socialist movement was split into disillusioned factions which only the devastation of war and the catalyst of the Bolshevik revolution would reunite and re-energise.

If the working-class and socialist movement enjoyed its 'heroic' years before World War One, as it has been said, it was nevertheless a revolutionary movement in its infancy. Almost every strategy was an exploration. Those that seemed to work were seized upon as the 'natural' course of the revolutionary process. As successive generations and different social and

40

occupational strata were drawn into the movement, a multiplicity of political and ideological tendencies became concrete social forces in opposition to each other. It was a development which offered real opportunities to non-socialist forces.

In the following chapter I will discuss how non-proletarian social groups used the socialist and working-class movements to facilitate their own political ascendence. And, in addition to a change within the structure of bourgeois politics, the newness of revolutionary socialist politics was manifested in an inadequate accounting of new ideological and political phenomena. It could not really be expected that Jules Guesde, who had been long and actively engaged in revolutionary struggle, should suddenly turn his attention to the threat posed by the emergence of a bourgeois social science. Nor should it have been expected that Jean Jaurès recognise the process of socio-political co-option in which he participated. But it was only in recognising these new developments and accounting for them in terms of their importance to revolutionary strategy that revolutionary analysis and philosophy could remain dynamic and critical.

It was the political independence of Georges Sorel that allowed him to give thought to developments which, while seeming peripheral to those people who were more immediately engaged in struggle, were actually the harbingers of future political problems. But, by elaborating a theory of socio-cultural integration, capitalist sociological science would ultimately contribute to the reform of the state school systems, refined approaches to political communications, and the social welfare programmes, which together have posed the contemporary question of the cultural and intellectual 'hegemony' of the ruling class.

The importance of Sorel's contribution to marxism lies in both his substantive critique of the new bourgeois sociology, and in his efforts to go beyond the vulgar determinism which generally passed for marxist philosophy in France before World War One. In addition, Sorel's direction of marxist praxis towards the question of proletarian consciousness in particular, and towards ideology in general, was the most abstract dimension of broader socio-cultural concerns which were based on his per-

41

ception of political trends in France. In contrast to the leaders of the major socialist parties, Sorel was not entirely optimistic about the imminence of socialist revolution. He saw the social forces of the capitalist system reacting instinctively in a powerful defensive reflex. From the rapid emergence of French sociology to the changing character of French politics, Sorel saw the marxist revolutionary praxis being undermined by a counter-revolutionary capitalist praxis it had helped to bring into being.

3. The Politics of Class Struggle: Against the Reproduction of Capitalist Polity

All too often when the history of the socialist movement and the development of marxism are discussed, it is done as if it can be understood outside the context of bourgeois political development itself. However, except for anarchist groups and their activities and the autonomous labour organisations like the *Bourses du Travail* and the C.G.T., the strategy and tactics of socialism in France were formulated in response to the attitudes and activities of the bourgeois parties and the state.

Of particular importance during the 1890s, when French socialism made its rapid electoral gains, was the emergence of a more socially liberal form of bourgeois electoral politics. And, just as the socialist movement represented a movement of class – of the working class plus a growing number of socially alienated bourgeois and petty-bourgeois intellectuals – so the new 'radical' politics represented a significant modification of the social structure. Behind the dramatic debates waged between the champions of 'socialism' and the defenders of the status quo during the early and middle years of the 1890s, was a deep-seated movement that might be compared to a sort of geological shifting between separate layers in the earth's crust. Accelerated industrial development not only shocked the working class into defensive positions, but it nurtured the rapid growth of the 'middle' classes, the functionaries, administrators, engineers, teachers and lawyers needed by the productive system and the new polity. Thus it was at precisely the same moment in modern French history that two major social groupings, the working class and the professional middle classes, began pushing for more influence within the French state.

In their simultaneous efforts to organise politically, both the working classes and the middle-class professionals had a history of political activity that can be traced far back into the

43

nineteenth century, but it was in the 1890s that they acquired a relatively high degree of socio-political self-awareness. The workers began to see their condition as the result of a system of oppression that must be overcome through struggle. The middle classes saw their condition as the result of their own efficient labours, and they believed that through manipulation of existing political means their authority could be increased. It was an ambiguous situation that led to confusion and mystification on both sides, as the antagonism between the interests of these two separate classes was not often realised at a time when they were *both* battling against the entrenched upper bourgeoisie. Thus the politics of early French socialism were greatly affected by the parallel development of a petty-bourgeois reformist politics (a tendency which was generally called 'radicalism' at the time). It was a challenge which quickly led the organised socialist parties into practical co-option and theoretical revisionism.

But if the decade between the beginning of the Dreyfus Affair in 1895 and the separation of church and state in 1905 saw the emergence of contradictions within the revolutionary social-ist movement, it was for these same reasons a period of creativity for Sorel. From his relatively detached position, Sorel saw more clearly the dynamic which worked to integrate socialist politics into the structure of capitalist polity. In addition, the fact that Sorel was formulating his interpretation of Marx's work and grappling with the tactical problems of French socialism at a time when liberal ideology was being transformed by changing relations between the classes, meant that the Sorelian variety of marxism emphasised the dialectics of ideological warfare. His thinking was characterised especially by a close attention to the attempts made by the French state to create a relatively homogeneous, supra-class political culture through its educa-tional institutions. Thus, Sorel's perceptions of the 'Radical Party' of the new middle classes, its political activities and its ideo-logy of 'social liberalism'[1] were centrally important in his assess-ment of socialist strategy and revolutionary potentialities in general.

Although a marxist, and thus conscious of how all culture and social behaviour in a class-divided society is essentially political in nature, Sorel had nothing but contempt for 'politics'

...s to hold themselves aloof from Dreyfusard agitation. ...e's vacillating response to the question later prompted Sorel ...that the Dreyfus Affair was 'the greatest event of our time' ... it was the 'experience which irrefutably established the ...ciency of the socialist theory then current'.[5] It was a period ...fusion which neutralised revolutionary forces to a certain ... and gave the reformist socialists under Jaurès (as well as ...dicals who profited most directly) an electoral impetus ... lasted until 1905 when Jaurès was forced to break with his ...al friends.[6]

...Finally, when the goverment of 'Republican Defence' was ...ed in June 1899, a government which included the socialist ...andre Millerand, Guesde broke with his hitherto socialist ... in the Chamber of Deputies saying: 'In leaving the group ...d the Socialist Union of the Chamber, which just helped the ...rgeois republic form a new government, the representatives ...rganised socialism and the working class . . . finish with a ...tics which is socialist in name only and which has been ...racterised by compromises and deviations that for a long time ...tried to displace with class politics . . . '[7] This in itself was a ...d decision, but even Guesde must have had to admit that ...newhere along the line he had been fooled. For Sorel, the ...air indicated how important the relation between theory and ...actice was – a socialist *praxis* must encourage an immediate ...tical assessment of new political developments rather than the ...rt of sluggishness and confusion that Guesde and the POF ...monstrated. Referring to the 'socialist writers' of his time and ...untry, Sorel concluded that 'these eminent thinkers were gener-...ly incapable of saying anything useful on questions not ...scussed by Marx or Engels'.[8]

It must be said however that there was no ready answer to the ...uestion of revolutionary tactics posed by the Dreyfus Affair. ...iven the circumstances (the degree of proletarianisation, the ...vel of revolutionary class consciousness, the degree of socio-...istorical understanding), there was no easily formulated or ...bvious tactic. The petty-bourgeois radicals were holding all the ...ards and would give no quarter to the conservatives. The danger ...or the socialists, from Sorel's perspective, was that if they tried to ...profit by the moral indignation being whipped-up by the radicals,

in the form of the compromise and opportunism which characterise parliamentary affairs. Most contemptible of these 'political' actors, in Sorel's estimation, were the petty bourgeois who animated the radical leagues and parties. He saw in them a lack of principle, an essential opportunism, which never ceased to amaze him.

Sorel recognised that the interaction between ideology and political behaviour was complex and changing from one historical epoch to another – that, in fact, very broad generalisations could be made along those lines. But in his work he paid close attention to the subtle characterological differences between individual politicians – differences that could herald shifts in political mentality and even ideology. For example, in spite of his contempt for the liberal coalition of 1898 under the bourgeois lawyer Waldeck-Rousseau, a government which was called the 'government of republican defence' (against a largely imaginary conservative threat), he contrasted Waldeck-Rousseau favourably with the radical politicians who succeeded him. While both bourgeois and reactionary, Waldeck-Rousseau nevertheless had great respect for constituted law and juridical principles. But such men were becoming more and more rare within the ranks of bourgeois politicians as the increasing demands made upon bourgeois politics encouraged expediency and a general atmosphere of hypocrisy and opportunism. It was a 'sign of the times', Sorel said, that opportunists like Waldeck-Rousseau were succeeded by politicians almost entirely devoid of principles.[2]

However, while there were differences between individual politicians which could be interpreted as 'signs of the times', these differences could not transform the general thrust of parliamentary politics in France: 'There are no essential differences between the various parties of the bourgeoisie. They have in common a cynical and profound contempt for people who do not seek to exploit the public treasury, a fear of socialism, and the same combative impulse to fight it with social reform.'[3] To fight socialism with social reform: this was perhaps the general realisation that lent the greatest critical importance to Sorel's political analysis. Reforms which *appeared* to be concessions wrought from an unwilling ruling class, could very well be part of a practical attempt to cut the ground from under the feet of the revolutionary movement. Sorel's consistent opposition to political programmes of social reform was ultimately based upon his calculation that such reforms would be used to dull class consciousness, that the reforms themselves would become the objective of working-class and socialist struggle. When Sorel denounced the 'socialists' in his writings, it was from this perspective.

The designation 'socialist' was, in fact, clear enough during the 1890s and after, when 'socialist' specifically meant those people associated with or supportive of one of the electoral parties. Those who stressed the primary importance of direct working-class action with a view towards the raising of proletarian consciousness as the overall revolutionary struggle were called 'revolutionary syndicalists' or 'anarcho-syndicalists', since their stress upon direct class struggle and non-participation in party politics distinguished them from the 'collectivists' who stressed centralised control and direction.

Sorel's concept of socialist revolution began and ended with the vision of a worker's struggle against the capitalist system – a struggle which could not be properly carried out within capitalist governmental institutions but which must use the only powers possessed by the working classes: their labour and their numbers. To Sorel, this position was not 'workerism', nor 'anarcho-syndicalism', nor an apolitical 'actionism'. It was rather a simple recognition that the socialist revolution would be the fruit of a proletarian struggle against the capitalist system and all its agents. But this was a very general premise. Of more immediate importance were questions of how the workers should wage the struggle on a practical day-to-day basis, and how they should respond to political developments. These were the tactical problems which demanded the kind of analytical perspective and critical inspiration that Sorel attempted to give the revolutionary movement.

In terms of both socialist theory and practical politics, the Dreyfus Affair was the most clearly defined political dilemma faced by the French socialist movement during the 1890s. The middle-class radicals posed the question in deceptively simple terms: a lower-rank army officer had been unjustly charged with and convicted of treason by officers and judges and with the complicity of certain politicians. This miscarriage of justice

46

occurred because of the blind arrogance class authorities, and the whole Affair irresponsibility with which the upper itself in political life.

What one was obliged to oppose attitude composed of upper-class snobber and individualism of classical *laissez faire* racist prejudices, the most outstanding current of anti-semitism. Thus the radica middle-class liberal professionals who w themselves politically against the conservati of Dreyfus' conviction in moral terms. It wa which caught their opponents off guard and among the socialists who realised naturally not the kind of issue which could directly se This does not include Jean Jaurès and the r who were closely allied to the radicals and whos centred around the social reforms that the rad which they used as bait in the formation of the in 1901. It was this union of the Radical and Party which led to a general election victory separation of church and state in 1905, the p objective of the radicals – involving as it did the the state education system.[4]

But for Jules Guesde and the collectivist rev the French Workers' Party (*Parti Ouvrier Françai* was immensely more difficult. The issue was bein radicals to embarrass a conservative and inflexible Undeniably the plight of Dreyfus was terrible, but h the POF go out on a limb? Should the concrete r demands of the working class be subordinated to t rhetoric of truth and justice that the radicals were u support against the government? Guesde found hi pletely disoriented by the advent of Dreyfusard agita recalled that at the beginning of the year 1898, when had just made his famous 'J'Accuse' declaration conde web of conspiracy and complicity surrounding th Dreyfus, Guesde was a 'more ardent Dreyfusard Jaurès'. But in July 1898 the POF issued a manifest by actively waging a similar campaign for the revision of Dreyfus' conviction, they would contribute to a deformation of working-class consciousness which would ultimately work against them. The very idea that a judicial error had been made, exceptional in nature, was an implicit affirmation of the system of justice. On the other hand the socialists certainly could not agitate *against* revision of the judge's decision. In the end it was perhaps best to let the radicals play out their strong hand while the socialists abstained, limiting themselves to critiques of the system of capitalist justice as a whole and mentioning Dreyfus within the context of the political contradictions within the ruling class. From this perspective, only a careful passivity could be counselled, and Sorel reacted much as did Fernand Pelloutier, who, as 'a petty-bourgeois intellectual attached to the cause of the people, assumed the contradictions of his situation' by condemning anti-semitism, acknowledging the courage of Emile Zola, approving the 'legitimate cry of indignation' of Jaurès, and asserting that the proletariat should not be actively involved in a conflict among the bourgeoisie.[9]

Although it was not until 1909 that Sorel published a work specifically dealing with the Dreyfus Affair and its importance for socio-political development in France, in 1903 he said, paraphrasing Rosa Luxemburg, that while 'the Dreyfus Affair brought us carloads of defenders of Truth, Justice and Progress' it was necessary 'to call upon heaven to protect [socialism] against its allies'. He concluded that 'contemporary socialism is sick because it has had too many friends'.[10]

With the publication of his *La Révolution dreyfusienne* in 1909, he transformed his observations into more formal analysis by linking the Dreyfusard movement with the general emergence of social liberalism in France. The Dreyfusards, he said, were the same people who advocated ameliorative social legislation for the purpose of pacifying an increasingly militant working class, and who used the philosophy of social liberalism to justify their actions to the bourgeoisie who (because of a more progressive tax scale) would pay for the reforms. The professional strata who constituted the ranks of the radicals would benefit most directly from such reforms – their political and social prominence would rise dramatically and the expansion of the state bureaucracy would increase their numbers and role in the management of the state.

Generally, Sorel explained how the Dreyfus Affair was a moment in a socio-political movement which involved the creation of a new class force with its own ideology within the capitalist polity. As such, the development must be viewed as a direct outcome of the transformation of capitalist production. The development of large scale industry not only created problems of control and regulation which increased the importance of the state and required the presence of technical and managerial personnel on an entirely new scale, but also accelerated the emergence of a wage-earning proletariat and, in turn, the organised working-class movement and socialism. It was this latter development which led to the emergence of classical bourgeois sociology. The capitalist polity needed the help of systematically obtained information and guidance in the formulation of state policies of social pacification.

Thus, the objective political and social conjuncture was more advantageous to an increase in the power of the new petty-bourgeois (or 'middle-class') cadres than it was to anything approximating proletarian revolution, *even if* the socialist and working-class movements were making strides that were historically unprecedented. It was a period that was particularly full of what could only be termed 'contradictions'. Even marxism itself, which was only just being introduced into France and diffused in one vulgarised form or another, was faced with the almost immediate danger of becoming isolated ideologically and ridiculed whenever it was dealt with. The new sociology thus represented a response of the ruling political structure to the emergence of a systematic opposition to the capitalist system which must be neutralised.

Sorel was not the only observer who recognised that the new discipline of sociology was part of a profound structural change, but he was unique in his ability to see the possible implications of recent developments which held only a one-dimensional aspect for most observers. While the emergence of sociological science might be a positive gain for human understanding in general, it had the potential of smothering alternative explanations of social process, such as marxism. The revision of

50

Dreyfus' condemnation was certainly desirable, but working for it could sap the strength of working-class struggle by casting a veil of liberal morality and ideology over the proletarian perspective. The ideological influence of the Catholic Church was bad, but to enlist socialist forces in the radical drive to separate church and state was to help the radicals to achieve political power and to gain control of the school system where they could install a new catechism, a 'civic' morality which would directly oppose the class realism upon which revolutionary proletarian consciousness rested. If ever revolutionary vigilance was required it was during the years 1895-1905 in France when new socio-occupational elites, convinced that they had science, truth and justice on their side, launched an offensive which was specifically calculated to co-opt socialist ideology and to condition the thinking of working people.

Sorel's awareness of how inadequate the 'official' marxism of the outstanding socialist leaders and parties was in providing creative guidelines for revolutionary action led him into the debate over 'revisionism'. The debate centred around the work of Eduard Bernstein and, ostensibly, it involved the 'revision' of the marxism practised by the major socialist leaders and parties in western Europe. The rather literal marxism of Guesde in France and Kautsky in Germany, which still placed a high value on the rhetoric of class struggle, was challenged by the new assessment of capitalist development made by Bernstein who said clearly that a proletarian revolution of a sudden, violent nature was out of the question. In effect, Bernstein buttressed with analysis what a growing faction within the German SPD and what reformist socialists like Jaurès in France were already practising: an electoral socialism committed to political compromise and the achievement of piecemeal reforms.

Sorel's reaction to the protagonists in this debate was confusing in the immediate context and it still can be considered ambiguous. Essentially, he was in agreement with the 'orthodox' marxists whenever they fell back on the idea of class struggle as an explanation of socio-political processes. But this tendency to 'fall back' on what constituted received ideas from almost infallible authorities – Marx and Engels – introduced a rigidity in their thinking and practice which tended to discredit the very

51

ideas they advanced. The reformists, and Bernstein in particular, seemed to react much more rapidly in the face of a rapidly changing capitalist productive system and polity. The emergence of the modern capitalist state with its increasingly sophisticated mechanisms for controlling class conflict, the growing successes of socialist electoral politics, and the expanding capitalist economies which seemed to promise an indefinitely rising general standard of living, all indicated to them that the end of capitalism would neither be soon nor of a 'catastrophic' nature; thus a reformist, gradualist approach to socialism seemed to be the only reasonable one. What Sorel accepted of the 'revisionist' analysis was its recognition of new developments within the capitalist system and its challenge to the rigidified 'orthodox' marxism. That he did not make an immediate political critique of revisionism was due to the fact that he was involved in his own polemic against orthodoxy. Tensions had developed between him and Paul Lafargue and Sorel virtually ceased to write for *Le Devenir social* during its last year of existence (1898). It was this break with Lafargue that led some observers to the mistaken conclusion that Sorel had joined the revisionists. In fact, he simply refused to choose between the dogma of the orthodox marxists and the opportunism of the revisionists.

Sorel saw a theoretical sterility in French socialism which had two main effects: firstly, all free discussion was coming to be considered as endangering the faith of the masses; and secondly, increasing authoritarianism emerged as efforts were made to maintain organisational and intellectual discipline. The vulgarisation of marxism represented by economic determinism was, therefore, primarily an effect of the growing authoritarian tendency within the socialist parties. In passing, Sorel pointed out again that Marx 'did not say that economic conditions are a *determining base*, but that productive relations (which, from the juridical point of view, are property relations) form the economic structure and the real base on which is raised the juridical and political super-structure'.[11]

The revisionists were correct in denying that the revolutionary process was an automatic one. Economic determinism not only denied the role of individual will in the revolutionary process, but it failed to account for the *ruling class's* own ability to *consciously*

52

wage the class struggle. The development of the state itself is much more than the reflex of a 'system'; it is part of a growing capitalist awareness of the changing nature of class politics. Bernstein, for example, maintained that the requirements of economic and technological transformation were determining less and less the transformation of other social institutions. As capitalism develops, Sorel stressed, the role of consciousness actually becomes more and more important. After the initial impact of industrial revolution, increasing control over mass consciousness becomes the most dynamic political factor in capitalist societies. The growing complexity of the capitalist state is in part a recognition of the need for cultural and ideological control over the working classes. Not only does the actual, physical capacity of the capitalist state grow and become more complex, but the level of awareness of its own function rises correspondingly. In a sense, then, capitalist praxis was becoming more subtle and self-conscious just at the time when marxist socialism was succumbing to the rigidification which comes from the bureaucratisation of political parties.[12]

Sorel saw in orthodox marxism the lingering traces of utopian socialism. The tenacity with which a fairly simplistic conception of historical and social development was gripped, indicated the presence of a less-than-rational faith in an historical destiny. On the other hand, he felt it was only fair to point out that marxist analysis had not really had enough time to be very well understood. Both 'orthodox' marxism and marxist 'revision-ism' could be explained as two unfortunate tendencies within the development of marxist thought; orthodoxy seized upon the dramatic conceptions of class struggle and catastrophic revol-ution in making a call to the workers and building their parties, while the revisionist reformers were not at all indisposed to recognise developments that seemingly ran counter to the prognostications made by the orthodox marxists. Sorel's own approach to marxist analysis was an attempt to synthesise these best elements of the two tendencies: to use the conceptual breakthroughs made by Marx – the idea of class struggle, the materialist conception of history – in a living manner which clarified new developments rather than rendering them less comprehensible.

53

It was apparent to Sorel that capitalism was entering a new phase of development, and he looked towards England in attempting to assess the direction which class struggle was likely to take. He noted that although there had been much open class struggle in England, the progress of capitalism had continued and it could be partially explained by a lack of proletarian solidarity. So, although the division between the classes is well-marked in England and social misery is visible everywhere, the force of a still powerful productive system gives it the semblance of omnipotence and a life-force which transcends the power of individuals. For many socialists, the perception of the British capitalist experience constitutes the basis of 'the ideology of fatalism *and* of liberty'. Fatalism, because the complexity of economic life and relations in the capitalist economy produces a feeling of being caught in an inextricable web of natural processes. On the other hand, while Marx correctly perceived that the capitalist development would ultimately have a liberating effect on working-class consciousness, he failed to take sufficient account of the strength of existing cultural norms. It is here, Sorel claimed, that 'Marx's research was quite incomplete. Living in a country [England] saturated with christianity, it seems as if he didn't really ask himself what the influence of moral education on the working classes was', nor did he sufficiently consider 'what relations exist between his conception of the class struggle and national traditions'.[13] Marx described clearly the objective processes of capitalist development, but what these underlying processes signify in terms of ideological and political conjunctures was a realm of analysis that later generations would have to take up, if an effective revolutionary strategy was to be formulated.

Sorel's thinking was caught between the same poles of fatalism and voluntarism that he referred to, tending to lean towards the former but balancing his thought with the awareness of the power of human volition. The idea of revolution itself incorporated contradictions which resulted in confusion and sometimes self-destructive political behaviour; and even the 'catastrophic' conception of revolution could be approached from different directions. While for Sorel the idea of fairly abrupt social and juridical transformation could be used as a social 'myth', as a vision of the objective of communal action, and thus be associated with the strategy of the general strike, many people become marxists for emotional reasons or because of a certain political immaturity. These individuals seize upon the idea of violent revolution as a sudden palliative for their own problems, which they project onto the society at large. The ambivalence in Sorel's own thinking was inherent in marxism, and it is possible that it could be resolved only at the risk of denying a part of the objective social and the subjective psychological reality that the revolutionary process involves. Sorel wished to see the end of the old utopian socialism because it could not adequately explain the reality of capitalist development; but on the other hand he wished to resuscitate and sustain the socialist vision and faith in the possibility and eventuality of socialist revolution. In a way, Sorel thus rejected both 'utopian socialism' and 'scientific socialism'. The former was based upon a chimerical optimism which naturally led to reformism and accomodation with the prevailing system of domination – good will taking the place of class struggle as the perceived social dynamic; while the expression 'scientific socialism' came quickly to be used (after the publication of Engels', *Socialism: Utopian and Scientific*, 1892) as a justification for not engaging in direct revolutionary action.

Regardless of its retention of marxist elements which suggest a revolutionary attitude, scientific socialism also involves a gradualist approach to social change in as much as it stresses the 'objective' factors of socio-historical development at the expense of the 'subjective'. The objective forces are seen as a steady, but slow-moving tide, but one that can be temporarily blocked by the subjective factors (actions of a spontaneous, or voluntaristic nature). The 'scientific' socialists fear that the slow unfolding of events will be interrupted. The pursuit of electoral politics as the revolutionary strategy is preferable to the kind of direct conflict between capital and labour that strikes, sabotage and boycotts represent, because it is tacitly assumed that the normal, uninterrupted workings of the system will inevitably create socialist pre-conditions in the shortest possible time. Direct and open conflicts on the other hand will more than likely spark off a reaction which will revive the prestige of established social authority, allow the imposition of repressive forms of

55

political control, and set back the revolutionary movement organisationally.

The attitude towards organisation itself marked the division between alternative conceptions of revolutionary struggle. The scientific socialists and the revisionists were both in favour of a developed party structure: Sorel, who as a revolutionary syndicalist favoured loose combinations of unionists without a rigid leadership structure or a bureaucracy, believed that formal organisation generally crippled the working-class movement because it tended to discourage local and individual creativity in the struggle. He generally tended to favour most direct actions against capital. Strikes, for example, if they are successful, increase the confidence of the workers; and if they are repressed intensify class hatreds. Of course this is a general position which leaves enormous room for extenuating circumstances and even direct contradictions; it remained for Sorel less of a positive recommendation than a rejection of the theoretical and practical rigidity of the marxist parties which dominated the revolutionary movement at the time.

Although Sorel considered himself above all to be a marxist, he nevertheless insisted that Marx's writings must be examined and used in the light of the contradictory elements existing within them. It would be absurd to believe that Marx's thinking did not change over time, that he remained subject to exactly the same philosophical influences and emphases throughout the decades of his literary production. It would be equally unwise to think that Marx offered one single strategic plan for the proletarian revolution. *The Communist Manifesto* for example, was written at a time when Marx and Engels were heavily influenced by Blanquist ideas, to the extent that a stress upon revolutionary party organisation can be found there.[14] But in Sorel's opinion the real importance of the document was its conception of the role of the proletarian class struggle in historical transformation. What was required in the 1890s, when major socialist groupings existed in western Europe and elsewhere, was a renewed research into the *questions* posed by Marx. Part of this task would involve the dissection of marxist concepts, a sorting out of the essential elements from those which reflected only the immediate influences on Marx as he wrote.

56

The work to do was enormous and could only be accomplished by a critical reading of Marx. Sorel, himself, was critical of Marx on a number of scores. For instance, he maintained that one of the weaknesses of modern socialist theory was its inadequate treatment of morality and religion. He claimed that Marx and Engels felt such considerations to be relatively unimportant because of the secularisation of thought, but that moral and religious habits of thought were continuing to play an undeniable role in the formation of working-class consciousness.[15] Or again, Sorel indicated that while the 'dialectical method' was obviously an advance in social and historical conceptualisation, it was by no means made explicit by Marx. Furthermore, the 'scientific' quality of marxism was open to question because, while Marx offered magnificent examples of *representation* in verifying his hypotheses, it was really beyond his capacity to *demonstrate* the proofs required of scientific laws. For example, in the case of the falling rate of profit, Marx was 'content to take empirical data and group them in a system, in giving them an apparently logical order'.[16] These criticisms, and others that Sorel made of Marx's work, were not designed to deprecate the importance of marxist thought. On the contrary, they were intended to help open the way to a more fruitful assimilation of it and a more creative application of the essentials of marxism to the problems faced by the proletarian movement.

Much of Sorel's own creative work (that is the work he did apart from criticising other marxists) was on the problem of proletarian consciousness. It is here that his discussion of revolutionary images as 'myths' figures as perhaps the most well-known of his conceptions. He conceived of politically motivated 'myths' as completely different from those totems, taboos or fantasies that the word is identified with today. 'Myths', Sorel stressed, are not 'utopias', and they are not 'descriptions of things', but rather the 'expressions of a will' to act on reality so as to change it. The 'myth' in question was the idea, or the vision, of class struggle leading to proletarian revolution; its most specific form was the idea of the general strike. This was a goal towards which the movement worked and which was realisable, but for which no time-table could be established. It was anything but an irrational element of mass pyschology, as many of Sorel's critics have maintained. On a purely psychological level, the general strike is 'the myth within which all of socialism is contained; that is, it involves a complex of images capable of naturally evoking all the feelings which are raised in the struggle of the socialist movement against contemporary society'.[17]

To encourage the acceptance of the myth of the general strike is therefore to encourage the acceptance of a whole complex of factors which combine to produce a revolutionary view of capitalist society. Most central is the idea of class struggle, a conception which simultaneously summarises the marxist view of capitalist society and indicates the direction which revolutionary action must take – the development of the proletariat's unique capacity to engage in combat with the capitalist ruling class. Seeking to reinforce this myth of the general strike as the culmination of class struggle is especially important for revolutionaries because of the growing capacity of the state to influence opinion and working-class consciousness: 'Our role [as revolutionaries]' Sorel said, 'can be useful in as much as we limit ourselves to combating bourgeois thought in such a manner as to alert the proletariat to the invasion of the ideas or the customs of the class enemy.' The role of the revolutionary intellectual is not to lead the revolutionary class struggle. That struggle is for the workers themselves to organise and carry out. Intellectuals should rather use their special talents 'to ruin the prestige of the bourgeois culture, the prestige which up until the present has opposed the principle of class struggle from fully developing within proletarian consciousness'.[18]

Sorel's idea of a social revolutionary myth was not irrational either in its conception or in its description of ideological development. The myth of the general strike required a certain leap of qualitative understanding, it is true; but it was the result of a realistic view of social reality and the imperatives of revolutionary change. On the other hand it was perhaps a poor explanation in that the word connoted too much an instinctive unconscious process. Sorel himself pointed out that his analysis of 'revolutionary myths' was founded upon the revelations of the 'new psychology' (undoubtedly that of Tarde, Le Bon and Bergson with their stress on collective reactions: imitation, crowd psychology and the 'élan vital').

58

After the Dreyfus Affair and the release of political energies which allowed the new middle-class professionals to form the Radical Party and achieve their electoral victory in 1902, the central political issue was the campaign to separate church and state. Once again it was an issue in which the consciousness of the working class was central. Although the petty-bourgeois radicals claimed that it was necessary to separate church from state primarily because of the influence the church exerted on politics from its advantageous position as demonstrated during the Dreyfus Affair, the real reasons were more immediate. In the first place, the radicals simply needed an issue with which to continue their electoral drive. The Dreyfus Affair had provided the perfect occasion to discredit the conservatives and to form a radical-moderate socialist alliance; now some other ideological issue was needed. But, secondly, the question of church and state was not merely artifical. The middle-class professionals had a positive interest in eliminating the church from the affairs of state. For one thing, the system of subsidised clerical schools limited the number of teaching positions open to the growing ranks of state functionaries. Finally there is the fact that the radicals were strongly ideological in their approach to politics. Given their position in the social structure, constituting the various levels of middle-class professional life, their interests were not as clear and stable as those of the propertied classes or of the working classes. Thus they identified strongly with the liberal principles of Jacobin democracy; individual initiative, civil liberties and the efficacy of the state. Above all, they considered themselves to be the rational backbone of social and political life. Tactically, the anti-clerical campaign allowed a more permanent alliance to be formed between the radicals and the moderate socialists.

From a reformist perspective the situation was promising. The radicals were committed to a programme of expanded state social services and they even talked of an inheritance tax. Their alliance with the socialists would surely benefit the workers in their struggles with private capital, at least indirectly. But from a revolutionary standpoint there was a real danger connected with the forceful ascendance of petty-bourgeois radical politics, especially with respect to working-class consciousness. In the short run many workers could be simply caught up in the

59

demagogically-waged electoral campaigns and could lose sight of the essential class nature of the interests camouflaged by the 'issues'. The long run consequences were potentially more serious. Once having separated church from state and reorganised the school system, the radicals would launch a programme of 'civic education' within the schools which would work directly against a realistic, class view of social relations and politics. Socialists, said Sorel, should take no pleasure from the radicals' attacks on the church, no matter how anti-clerical they were themselves. 'When the republican state resolved to establish a secular education for the masses', he said, 'it was not acting from purely ideological motives; the end in view was very immediate and completely concrete.' The radicals wished to 'teach succeeding generations to form a single conception of the Republic, the nation, and France'.[19]

Sorel's alarm was well-founded. Already, long before they actually were able to form a government and go about the business of bringing state education into line with the new political – ideological – requirements of an industrial capitalist society, the radicals had been attempting to 'educate' workers away from thinking in terms of class interests. In 1897, radical university professors, teachers and others were instrumental in creating the 'popular universities', private institutions modelled on the English system of university extension and the 'working men's clubs'. The educational content of these schools was definitely bourgeois in the sense that it reflected the course content at the state universities and, as the chief administrator of the popular universities pointed out, 'we are of the people and we wish to remain of the people, but we would be happy to contribute to a reconciliation between the social classes'.[20] These popular universities were founded throughout France and the movement existed for a good decade (up until around 1910). They were tangible evidence of what the rising social liberals of the capitalist state, the middle-class professionals who activated radical politics, were preparing for the working class. It was a warning that the major problem that revolutionaries in particular and the proletariat in general would face would be the effort to establish against them what Gramsci would eventually call the 'intellectual hegemony' of the ruling class.

In the largest sense, Sorel saw all these developments as the surface signs that the productive system had become much more complex than most marxists had realised. Not only was direct competition between capitalist enterprises being managed by the private companies themselves or regulated by the state, thus presenting a relatively monolithic combination of capitalist forces in the face of the working-class movement, but the social structure itself was becoming more complex, instead of simplifying, as those who anxiously waited for the petty bourgeoisie to fall into the proletariat expected on the basis of Marx and Engels' remarks in the *Communist Manifesto*. Sorel observed that capitalist development was producing 'a real variety of social strata' which was blurring the old class lines, while at the same time 'political parties are attempting more and more to dissimulate material interests through the use of ideology'.[21] Thus, corresponding to the emergence of new social groups and new social relations within the capitalist system, was the emergence of a new political situation. A bourgeois politics of authority and repression was being replaced by an effort to elicit practical co-operation and ideological consensus.

The difference between clerical education and secular, state education was in fact heavy with political implications. Whereas the church spoke from a position of authority and presumed to hand down moral rules, the state teachers explained how the system of republican governments was the most rational possible and how particular interests, including those of separate social classes, must conform to the interests of the majority, embodied in the state. But while Sorel could detect the political tendencies active in France with a fair degree of accuracy, he was not able to say exactly what the results of the new form of bourgeois politics would be. On the one hand he allowed himself to say (in 1903) that the workers 'don't fall for such masquerades after they have been exposed to socialist propaganda'.[22] But given the lack of an effective socialist counter-education, a certain pessimism could be justified just as easily. Social behaviour simply could not be predicted in the light of the increased importance of ideological conditioning.

It was natural that Sorel should pay a certain amount of attention to the question of 'fatalism and liberty' as he attempted

61

to clarify the essentials of marxism and to apply them in analysing prevailing socio-political conditions. Having never embraced the blind spontaneity of the anarchists, and refusing to lapse into the cut-and-dried determinism of the outstanding 'marxists' of his day, through necessity he tempered an objective and uncompromising account of the difficulties presented to the proletarian movement with an affirmation of the potential of conscious human action to change history. In marxist 'revision-ism' he saw a refreshing willingness to take an objective look at changing conditions and to reject out-moded conceptions as a result of it. Yet what the revisionists rejected, namely the marxist conception of revolutionary class struggle, was the very essence of marxism. And if the 'orthodox' marxists retained the central notion of class struggle, it became rigidified and unsubtle in their thinking, greatly reducing the effectiveness of marxist analysis as a foundation for revolutionary strategy and tactics. The weak-nesses of both revisionism and orthodox marxism derived in part from the dynamic of party organisation and electoral politics. The reformist revisionists wished to spread their electoral net as widely as possible by offending the least number of people with class-against-class rhetoric, while the orthodox marxist parties strove to attain an internal doctrinal consensus. In both cases a reproduction of the capitalist polity occurred. The revisionists tended to hide class interests under an illusion of the general common interest – a central element of liberal capitalist ideology – while the orthodox marxists tended to become authoritarian in their approach to both doctrinal and practical questions of socialist organisation and strategy. It was the temptation to follow the electoral road which deflected socialist revolutionaries from a revolutionary proletarian strategy, into one whereby socialist 'intellectuals' would spearhead an attempt to capture and then use the state.

Sorel's marxism began with the proposition that a prole-tarian revolution would result from the class-conscious action of the proletariat. The development of revolutionary class con-sciousness was thus the proper work of all socialist revolution-aries. Strategy and tactics would, therefore, be evaluated on the basis of whether or not they contributed to or detracted from that development. Sorel's analysis of the Dreyfus Affair and the

62

campaign to separate church from state began with an effort to explain the events in objective, structural terms – to show how they were political phenomena with class-based origins. New social strata, the increasing numbers of middle-class professionals created by the advent of industrial capitalism in France, were forging a new political situation. An institutionalised 'social liberalism' was coming to pose a challenge to the revolutionary movement that only a sophisticated and fluid marxism could account for.

4. The Revolutionary *Syndicats* and the General Strike

In 1905, Sorel declared flatly that 'revolutionary syndicalism' is the practical realisation of what is truly essential in marxism. For him, it was an expression of marxism 'superior to any and all theoretical formulations', because it expressed the class struggle in a conscious, militant and direct fashion.[1] Then, as now, this position was far from the conventional socialist wisdom. To place one's hopes for revolution in something which smacks of what came to be called 'workerism' seems a denial of both analytical subtlety and practical common sense. But a revolutionary movement advances primarily by learning through experience how to avoid the mistakes it has made in the past. And it was through his analysis of the tactics of the working-class and socialist movements that Sorel came to endorse the attitudes, ideas and everyday socialist practice of 'revolutionary syndicalism'.

Revolutionary syndicalism was an organised movement of the working class which emerged in France during the 1890s. In general it was a rather spontaneous and natural development in which conscious and militant workers combined an organised strategy of proletarian defence with a militant understanding of the marxist vision of class struggle. The most important two characteristics of revolutionary syndicalism in France were firstly that it was a movement *of* the working class which was *autonomous* – unconnected with the socialist parties, and secondly that it was revolutionary in the sense that strikes, demonstrations and other forms of struggle were considered as stages or moments in a long-term revolutionary struggle of a class nature leading to the overthrow of the capitalist system. Revolutionary syndicalism was thus sharply distinguished from pacific British trade unionism and the labour movement in Germany which was organically connected with the German Social Democratic

64

Party. Only the I.W.W. in the United States achieved a similar degree of political autonomy and revolutionary spirit.

Revolutionary syndicalism in France emerged quickly and with quite a high level of political consciousness. In a way it was a delayed reaction created by the bloody 'birth' of the Third French Republic, which involved the brutal suppression of the Paris Commune in 1871 and subsequent repression continuing far into the 1880s. Not only were many of the most militant workers slaughtered in the Franco-Prussian War or in the Commune, but others were exiled or forced into inaction by the new regime. Socialist organisations could survive only as secret societies until 1876, while formal labour organisation was illegal until 1884. It is therefore understandable that socialist organisation in France first assumed a strictly political aspect and was conceived in essentially centralist or 'collectivist' terms. On the other hand, socialism in France was decidedly 'revolutionary' at this time. The various socialist organisations expressed, almost without exception, a belief in the impending, thorough, and probably violent destruction of bourgeois society. Due to the conditions of its germination – rapid industrialisation and economic distress in general – the French socialist movement came out of the 1880s very messianic and revolutionary in tone.

As the decade ended, however, the French socialist movement experienced a series of events which greatly complicated the tactical and strategic choices it was faced with. In fact, two main roads opened up: electoral politics, and direct action against capital – strikes. Although labour stoppages had long been a natural and frequent manifestation of working-class defence, it was only during the late 1880s, after the legalisation of labour organisation, the return of the Communards and the execution in 1887 of American revolutionaries after the Haymarket Affair, that the strike began to be considered as a political weapon, a conscious tactic of class war. The idea of a general strike in particular rapidly gained popularity in militant working-class circles, first timidly broached at the Second Congress of Workers' *Syndicats* in 1887 and then formally adopted by the congress in 1888. The idea also gained support at the Socialist Congress at Troyes in September, 1888. Part of this growing realisation of working-class power was the adoption of the date May the First,

65

as a workers' holiday during which work would stop and workers the world over would demonstrate in favour of an eight hour day. In France this event was decided upon at the International Socialist Congress held in Paris in July, 1889. During these years there was little opposition to the idea among socialists, although Frederick Engels wrote to Laura Lafargue in May 1890 that Jules Guesde was wrong to endorse the idea and did so because of his former attraction to anarchism. In fact, Guesde had no reason to oppose a measure which was at once an expression of a growing working-class self-confidence and an undoubted stimulus to action.

In 1889 there did not seem to exist any major contradiction between direct working-class action and socialist electoral politics. It was all part of one general movement against the bourgeoisie and capitalism. However, the attitude of the major socialist parties was to change totally during the first few years of the 1890s. Entering electoral lists in the 1880s was a means of ending the isolation of the socialists from the political process and thus from the possibility of immediately helping to alleviate the condition of the working masses. The population was clearly becoming more and more desirous of radical change; and it was this radicalisation which the socialists hoped to channel and enlarge upon through the vehicle of universal manhood suffrage – the bourgeois republic's own institution. Their hopes were almost immediately rewarded. The French Workers' Party (*Parti Ouvrier Français*) of Jules Guesde and Paul Lafargue, for example, went from being a small sect in 1890 to 'the first and foremost party of the modern type in France' by 1893.[2] It had great success in mobilising support for the May Day holidays in 1890 and 1891 and its membership grew rapidly, from 2,000 members in 1889 to 10,000 in 1893. In the legislative elections of 1889 it received 25,000 votes; in 1893 it received 160,000.

This growing electoral success naturally influenced the social perspective of many socialists. Perhaps instead of a Great Day of Reckoning, a mortal combat between Capital and Labour, the dawn of socialism would break after a longer, more peaceful process of elections and legislation. Thus it has been said that the 'tonality' of the revolutionary atmosphere was completely different after 1892.[3] It is equally just to say that it was not until the 1890s that the great contemporary questions of the socialist movement were first posed in France: What actual role would the working classes play in the struggle against capitalism? What attitude should revolutionaries take *vis à vis* the state? What tactics should be central in the building of class cohesiveness and revolutionary consciousness?

These questions were posed even more starkly in the early 1890s because of the wave of anarchist terrorism which broke loose. Terrorist activity forced virtually all the parliamentary socialists to dissociate themselves from 'direct' or 'violent' tactics. Autonomous working-class organisations emerged at the same time, and it was the very issue of 'direct action' tactics, the general strike in particular, which caused enough dissension within the international worker congresses to end the tutelage over the Federation of *Syndicats* and other groups which the socialist parties had exerted. Revolutionary syndicalism came into existence when the first *Bourses du Travail* (labour exchanges) opened in 1892 and then fused with the Federation of *Syndicats* in 1895 to form the General Federation of Labour (*Confédération Générale de Travail*), a purely proletarian organisation which divorced itself from the socialist political parties. The movement grew rapidly. In 1900 there were 57 *bourses* and 1,000 *syndicats*, and by 1908 more than 150 *bourses* and more than 2,000 *syndicats*. Its activities and communications were numerous and varied and it can easily be said that, up until World War One, the current of revolutionary syndicalism which powered the C.G.T. was *the* revolutionary movement in France.

In considering Sorel's conception of revolutionary syndicalism, it must be understood that he should not be considered a 'theorist' of the movement. What came to be called 'revolutionary syndicalism' in France became an ideological tendency only when the practice of it began to be rejected by those who claimed to be able to advance the proletarian cause through other methods. For Sorel, as for the other major figures associated with revolutionary syndicalism, its premises were deeply rooted in the material reality of capitalist society; it was in no way the emanation of an idea. Revolutionary syndicalism, he said, 'bears the same relation to the class struggle that capitalism bears to competition between private interests – pushed by a powerful instinct to produce as much action as the material conditions permit'. As a marxist, Sorel considered the necessity of proletarian organisation and revolutionary activity the first premise of any socialist revolutionary thought. Questions concerning the devising of strategy and the development of a more general revolutionary consciousness remain, but a marxist begins by assuming that socialism will be the result of a necessary praxis of the proletariat, not the result of an idea. 'Today, revolutionary syndicalism represents that which is most powerful in marxism and superior to all formulas: to know that the class struggle is the alpha and omega of socialism – that it is not a sociological concept thrown around by professors, but an ideological aspect of a social war being carried out by the proletariat against the captains of industry – that the *syndicat* is the instrument of the social war.'[4] In short, revolutionary syndicalism is 'proletarian socialism' – as opposed to petty-bourgeois socialism or political socialism, the socialism of the intellectuals.

Throughout Sorel's written work lies the assumption that a proletarian revolution must be made by the proletariat, that it cannot rely upon other social groups or certain individuals to 'lead' it or to 'educate' it. In addition, it went almost without saying that the proletariat must be organised for struggle. Thus the 'theoretical' and, we can say in the same breath, the 'practical' position of revolutionary syndicalism was merely to stress the priority of encouraging the proletariat, by all possible means, to organise and act in accordance with revolutionary objectives. Never, it must be emphasised, did Sorel claim that socialist political activity was *essentially* bad and thus absolutely undesirable. He maintained, with force and often with vehemence, that such political activity should subordinate itself to the direct struggle between the proletariat and capital. The problem, as he saw it, was that the reverse occurred: the parliamentary socialists subordinated the struggle of the proletariat to that of the socialist politicians (or, we could say, the politicians to a large extent substituted the electoral struggle for direct combat against the capitalist mode of production).

It is equally important to realise that both the socialist politicans and the revolutionary syndicalists claimed that their strategies derived directly from the concepts and new understandings found in marxism. It was not a time when 'marxism' was an ideological red herring associated with particular parties or existing social structures. Even the anarchists of the time had no special aversion to Marx's analysis of capitalist society and his description of the broad parameters of the road to socialist revolution. The task was the proper application of the conceptual breakthroughs pioneered by Marx to the reality of proletarian struggle. The end in view was not the modification of capitalist practice so as to improve the relative lot of the workers within the capitalist system of production, but rather to build the social foundation of a new kind of society while working to destroy the old. When Sorel turned his attention directly to the social and historical significance of syndicalism, it was to discuss it as an agent of revolutionary historical change and as the seedbed of a new society. His major work on the *syndicats* was appropriately entitled 'The Socialist Future of the *Syndicats*', for in his conception their primary importance lay in their work of revolutionary transformation. In this long and often-reprinted article he wished in the first instance 'to call attention to certain theoretical points of view and show how Marx's historical materialism illuminated these problems'; then, he continued, 'when the works of Marx and Engels are more available to the French public, I will discuss the theory of the revolutionary proletariat'.

It was precisely this 'theory of the revolutionary proletariat' which activated the polemics around the interpretation of Marx's writings. To Sorel, it seemed as if the vast majority of French marxists were making a fundamental error as they sought to infuse their socialist praxis with marxist analysis. 'We know', he observed,

> with how much energy the marxist school has insisted on the impossibility of making a social revolution before capitalism has sufficiently developed; it is because of this thesis that the marxists have been accused of fatalism, because it severely limits the importance of subjective thought and action – even when material factors are subordinate to rational action. It seems that all too often what Marx wrote has been read superficially. For example,

69

all his disciples say that the revolution can only be the work of the proletariat and that the proletariat is the product of large-scale industry, but they are not sufficiently aware that Marx meant also that the working classes must acquire the juridical and political capacity [to consciously make a revolution] before being able to turn to triumph.[5]

For Sorel there was nothing at all superficial or mechanistic about Marx's analytical work; but that 'marxist school' as it had developed and was developing in France had extracted from Marx a decidedly deterministic view, not only of the development of capitalism, but also of the development of the proletariat's capacity to make a revolution. In effect, the approach of the 'marxist school' was deterministic and fatalistic, because, as Sorel pointed out, it revealed a basic lack of confidence in the proletariat's ability to learn from its collective and individual experience and to turn that knowledge into a rational programme of revolutionary action. To Sorel, it was evident that, regardless of how propitious the 'objective' conditions were for proletarian revolution, there could be no revolution in the profound social sense unless the proletariat had already made a *subjective* revolution in the form of a transformed social consciousness. Regardless of how much it was agreed that it was the proletariat which would ultimately make the revolution, the fact that the proletariat could not help but be influenced by the leaders of the socialist movement meant that the proper interpretation of Marx's work was of great importance. It was more than a theoretical debate between rival sectarians – it was a political struggle between differing social groups and ideological tendencies within the actual current of social transformation.

Sorel maintained one primary assumption in this analysis: the fact that analysis itself – or 'theory' as intellectuals prefer to call it – must be informed by practice.

When *direct action* has demonstrated its effectiveness, the people who have disinterestedly hoped that socialism would renew the world will use their creative faculties to sketch a programme of working-class movement which will be adapted to this form (direct proletarian action) of working-class struggle. These analysts will observe that there are

70

very intimate connections between syndicalist ideology and that which is most original in Marx's work; and thus the most legitimate revision of marxism will be realised.[6]

In an important way, the controversies which then raged in socialist circles were encouraged by a lack of properly planned and executed proletarian action. Indeed, the central controversy was over the 'revisionist' ideas of Eduard Bernstein, whose analysis of capitalist development led him to dismiss direct working-class action entirely. Bernstein argued openly against the phenomenon of autonomous proletarian organisation and action, which he called 'workerism'. Equally he challenged the very idea of the existence of a 'proletariat', pointing out that it was in the most developed industries where class consciousness was weakest.[7] In the manner of the academic sociologists, Bernstein encouraged the notion that class differences were destined to disappear and that, consequently, the only possible role for socialist development was on the electoral stage, where the goals would necessarily be ameliorative and essentially reformist, rather than revolutionary. Syndicalist action would have to conform to the political programmes of the parliamentary socialists; it would become, in fact, their political tool.

The difficulties faced by the revolutionary syndicalist movement were, therefore, considerable. Not only was there the vast work of encouraging the workers in general to look at their situation clearly and to develop a sense of their role in historical development. There was also the additional necessity of opposing the relatively well-organised and articulate champions of parliamentary socialism. Sorel generally viewed this as a tendency towards 'social pacifism' which conceived of 'politics' as founded upon the notion of 'equilibrium'. It was exactly this politics of 'equilibrium', or accommodation, that a movement powered by the perception of a necessary class struggle must try to overcome. In this context, Sorel believed that direct action, the strike in particular, was absolutely essential. He claimed that, just as wars engender or help to develop nationalist sentiments, so local and frequent strikes can reinforce socialist sentiments, encourage a spirit of self-sacrifice, and work to keep the vision of revolution alive. Sorel qualified these basic strategic considerations by

71

saying that it was imperative that in the course of strikes and related activities, the anger felt and expressed by workers should not result in injury to other workers or to the public at large. Sabotage, for example, must always affect the bosses, and not the public. The question of 'terrorism' was evidently a moot one. It was only a few years before Sorel wrote his article on 'The Socialist Future of the *Syndicats*' that the wave of anarchist 'propaganda by the deed' showed that not all direct action was progressive. The effect of *that* form of direct action was merely the discrediting of much of the content of the anarchist movement, *plus* the passage of a large amount of special repressive legislation. The years of that experience demonstrated fairly conclusively that the bourgeois state could not be blackmailed into submission, and that workers did not gain a developed class consciousness by the spectacle of 'deeds of propaganda' (or 'exemplary actions' as they are called today).

Regardless of Sorel's conviction that a true social war must be carried out by the *syndicats*, it was obvious to him that in a country with a democratic political system 'an infinite number of complications make it impossible to maintain a state of war in all dimensions of life'. On the level of 'public opinion', for example, the bourgeois press wielded enormous power. Events had demonstrated that the working class could be deflected from a proper consideration of its own interests on questions of foreign affairs, civil liberties and anti-clericism. Sorel simply noted that the Dreyfus Affair was 'too recent to have to insist on this point'. And the point was that the struggle of the workers must remain focused upon clear revolutionary goals: the building of revolutionary consciousness and organisation. Attempting to subsume proletarian interests within general 'progressive' or 'democratic' goals could only have the effect of obscuring social relations and strategic revolutionary priorities.

The capitalist legislatures were constantly devising new laws which ostensibly afforded workers more protection. The parliamentary socialists unceasingly agitated to incline capitalist jurisprudence in a direction more favourable to the workers; and the socialist press made a constant pitch to bourgeois opinion by appealing to sentiments of goodwill, humanity, solidarity – in short, to bourgeois morality. Sorel did not say that all this

72

activity was absolutely bad, but he was uncompromising in his condemnation of the effects of it, especially given the apparent desire of the political socialists to constitute their reformist politics as the revolutionary process itself.

The combined effort of the clerical and state schools to form the thinking of the working class was another difficulty facing the revolutionary syndicalist movement. 'It is especially through the use of books', Sorel pointed out, 'that the proletariat is placed under the spell of an ideology which is foreign to it.' Given the structure and strictures of the state system of education, little could be done directly to eliminate this psychological aspect of the capitalist state's anti-revolutionary activity. Sorel deplored the fact that France so sadly lacked a 'good socialist literature'.[8] It perhaps occurred to him that the socialist intellectuals might use their energies and skills to better advantage if they endeavoured to provide the proletariat with such a revolutionary literature, rather than reproducing capitalist politics.

In the final analysis Sorel felt that the future of the revolutionary movement depended almost solely on the success of revolutionary syndicalism – on the revolutionary activity of the proletariat itself. Any *diminishing* of what revolutionary class consciousness existed among the proletariat would mean simply that the overturning of the capitalist system would be that much more difficult, regardless of how much social legislation was passed through the efforts of parliamentary socialists and capitalist reformers. In 1898, and for some years after, Sorel was apprehensive about the advances of this 'social pacifism'. 'When we think about these things', he said, 'we must say that the fusion of social classes dreamed of by the social Catholics and the radicals is perhaps not as absurd an idea as we at first thought. It is not impossible that socialism could disappear as a result of a *reinforcement of democracy*, if revolutionary syndicalism was not there to combat this "social peace".'[9]

Yet Sorel remained hopeful that the new spirit and organisation which had emerged in France would be able to resist and override these counter-revolutionary tendencies, and he went on to say that the syndicalist movement appeared to be succeeding in raising the militancy of the struggle in the same degree that social concessions were made to the workers. But this was written

73

at a time when the syndicalist movement was relatively fresh and dynamic, when Fernand Pelloutier was still alive and when the militant workers had not been deflected from their revolutionary path by socialist reformers or beaten down by government repression. The counter-tendencies Sorel noted would loom even more ominously during the years immediately preceding World War One.

The general tasks of revolutionary syndicalism revolved around three essential questions, three questions which were in fact the central concerns of all marxist revolutionaries: Firstly, has the proletariat acquired a clear consciousness of its existence as a class culturally autonomous from others and with interests antagonistic to those of the capitalist bourgeoisie? Secondly, is the proletariat strong enough to act in concert against the capitalist classes? And thirdly, is the proletariat engaged in the work of resisting capitalist ideology and eliminating it from its thinking while it endeavours to overthrow the capitalist system of production? For Sorel, these questions indicated what the essential tasks of the revolutionary movement should be: working-class organisation should be pursued with the development of revolutionary class consciousness as the primary goal. This would necessarily involve the encouragement of a sense of working-class cultural autonomy – a focusing upon the basic psychological, behavioural and ethical differences between the social classes – especially those between the workers and the bourgeoisie. The character of intermediary classes would and should, according to Sorel, be explained in terms of their location between the classes. Contact between the proletariat and those individuals with non-proletarian social origins should be revolutionary contact; that is non-proletarian revolutionaries should approach the proletariat in a spirit of recognising the essential value and revolutionary necessity of proletarian culture. Revolutionaries with bourgeois or petty-bourgeois origins should endeavour to help workers to understand the function of those institutions so that they could be more effectively combated.

Sorel used the example of the various sorts of 'mutual aid' societies, co-operatives of various sorts, especially financial ones, that had emerged as a response to the rapid proletarianisation of the French working classes. These organisations could take on

74

very different characters depending upon who founded them and what ties they had to capitalist economic processes. The most important evaluation that could be made of them was whether or not they could exist within the syndicalist network, and which of them were essentially capitalist institutions. The latter posed a positive threat to the revolutionary conception of syndicalism and working-class autonomy. The importance of this question of principle must not be doubted.

> Reducing the *syndicats* to the status of being only defensive organisations is to throw up a formidable barrier in the way of proletarian development. It is to expose and subject the proletariat to the powerful influence of bourgeois demagogues while reducing the importance of the economic forces which can contribute to the maintenance of working-class autonomy. It is to impede the elaboration of the new principles which must emerge organically from working-class life – juridical principles of its own. It is, in short, to refuse the proletariat the possibility of becoming a class *for itself*. The mutual aid societies founded by the *syndicats* do not work in the least upon the same principles as the bourgeois savings banks; instead of inspiring the investment of capital, they maintain the development of proletarian solidarity.[10]

The general point was that working-class co-operatives of any sort could be either reactionary or progressive, depending on the context and the ends foreseen. Co-operation could either 'facilitate or obstruct the proletarian movement'.[11]

Revolutionary syndicalism was, therefore, far more than what has become known as 'unionism'. Its goals were not immediate, involving wage rises and improved working conditions, nor even more long-term measures such as the creation of a full-blown state system of social security. Working-class organisation was considered as the essential means towards a *revolutionary* goal – the eventual dismantling of capitalist production and the social relations which made it possible. Of first importance in this process was the development of an awareness of the necessity of such a revolution among the proletariat itself.

Without such an informed social consciousness there would not and could not be a true proletarian revolution.

The creation of this consciousness could not, equally, be the work of people foreign to the working classes, although such people could play a role in the development of the proletariat's ability to *inform itself*. The content of an autonomous proletarian culture would be, most importantly, a juridical-ethical perspective which could not encompass capitalist values and practice. Egotistical individualism, dog-eat-dog competitiveness, the hypocrisy of meting out justice along class lines while proclaiming equality before the law – these things would have to be seen clearly by workers, and rejected in favour of socially equitable standards of justice and human conduct. If the proletariat could achieve this kind and level of consciousness, then it would possess a sophisticated and self-conscious culture of its own. In the same measure, the foundations of a socialist society would exist; for the meaning of revolution lies in the emergence of new, formal and informal, social relations. This is the 'cultural' work of revolution which must precede any serious physical attempt to overturn the capitalist system.

Sorel made it clear that his assessment of the historical task of revolutionary syndicalism was in no way based solely upon his own observations: 'Marx's thought cannot be doubted – the transformation must be made by a mechanism within the very bosom of the proletariat, it is by means of its own resources that it must create the new ethos' – the new socio-juridical consciousness. It is important to realise, however, that neither Marx nor Sorel advocated the political isolation of the proletariat; that would have been to take an essentially defensive stance in the face of capitalist institutions. Electoral politics were, for example, not at all ruled out of the revolutionary movement, but their role – and the goals sought by them – must be supportive of the development of proletarian consciousness and culture. 'What must be sought from the public powers', Sorel said, 'are the facilities with which the people can proceed by themselves with this work of transformation. It is with this objective that workers [should] be engaged in electoral politics. The practice of such political struggle is therefore quite clear, and it is not necessary to pose some arbitrary or *ideal* objectives, as do the 'political'

76

revolutionaries.'[12] The real revolutionary objective unites socialist ideals in respect of the farthest reaching vision of the new
society, with the practical, everyday tasks at hand; it is to
encourage the development of a culture which takes the example
of capitalist thinking and practice as *its negative point of
departure* in the building of a new basis for human relations. In
building the revolutionary movement, Sorel said, we should be
trying to identify how modern capitalist production attempts to
enclose the proletariat within a capitalist juridical-ethical frame
of reference.

Yet the goal of revolutionaries is in no way a mere attempt
to preserve what were essentially pre-capitalist ethics. It must be,
rather, a 'post-capitalist' ethic informed by the experience of
proletarianisation: 'Like Marx, we take the organisations
designed as defences against capitalism as our point of departure.
What we ask ourselves is whether these coalitions have not given
rise among workers to juridical principles which are in contradiction with traditional principles.'[13] Sorel, of course, assumed
that the process of socialisation which capitalism engendered on
virtually every level of life did involve the general creation of a new
perception of social responsibility which, if it became self-
conscious, would constitute a revolutionary value-system.

As a result of this growing self-awareness, workers would
turn their defensive organisations into offensive revolutionary
weapons. But the transformation would be a difficult one,
involving the rejection of capitalist ideology in its most subtle
forms. The very idea of delegating authority, for example, would
have to be examined carefully. Sorel strenuously opposed what
he termed the 'democratic principle' derived (at least on the level
of abstract thought) from Rousseau's 'general will', which
presumes a delegation of authority from the rank and file to a set
of union officials who carefully stake out their right to make
decisions for the rank and file, and then impose those decisions on
them. Sorel did not make clear exactly how decisions should be
made within the *syndicats*, merely stating as a matter of general
principle that the workers should not be removed from the
decision-making process to the degree that individuals participate only indirectly.

It also went almost without saying that the *syndicats* should

77

have no formal relations with political parties. From a revolutionary point of view such autonomy was a positive benefit to the parties themselves, as the presence and actions of the *syndicats* worked a constant pressure on politicians to contest the legislative compromises which characterise the legislative process. In addition, the presence of the *syndicats* encouraged ambitious socialist politicians to assume more revolutionary positions than those maintained by politicians already elected. Within factories and workshops the *syndicats* should strive to win as much authority in their own supervision as possible. If, for example, a call was made for more supervisory personnel, they should agitate for the right to perform these functions for themselves. These things should be done with no illusions; for neither electoral politics nor a progressive worker 'self-management' would end the capitalist mode of production. But the workers must, through the *syndicats*, increase their confidence and consciousness by flexing their muscles and extending their influence with each opportunity that arises. Better still they must make their own opportunities.

The ways in which the *syndicats* would work their influence were, therefore, very diverse. The co-operatives, Sorel hoped and expected, would be inspired by the example of class consciousness and solidarity evident in the *syndicats*:

> The *syndicats* can exert a great influence on the co-operatives to the point of dictating the direction they will take, especially at the moment of their formation. It is up to the *syndicats* to animate them with the proletarian spirit, to keep them from turning into simple economic relief societies and to encourage the elimination of anything which smacks of capitalist enterprise from them. What is really essential to elicit from the co-operatives is the development of new juridical conceptions. For example, conceptions such as 'seller-buyer' and 'loaner-borrower', which dominate the lives of workers in their relations with shopkeepers, should give way before conceptions involving co-operation and solidarity.[14]

The idea was not to build barriers between bourgeois institutions

78

and ideology on the one hand and the proletariat on the other, but rather to combat capitalism on every level with organisation and a view of what is right and just that is properly proletarian. The workers would be foolish to refuse the help of individuals and groups with non-proletarian origins, but the fight against capitalist production and social relations was essentially their fight. To consent to be 'led' by anyone (or any party) would, in effect, be an abdication of their will and capacity to struggle for their own, proletarian, revolution.

The mechanics of that revolution were hard to foresee, and Sorel at no time attempted to outline a detailed revolutionary strategy. He was, however, very clear about the essential path the revolutionary movement would take. The working classes would make their own revolution through the use of the enormous power they possessed: their labour. A system founded upon the organisation and exploitation of human labour is potentially at the mercy of this indispensable element of its operation. Should labour be withheld from production, all the political and cultural edifices built upon it would crack and crumble. In outline, the strategy was simple: working-class organisations must be broadened and deepened to the extent that such a common action was possible, and proletarian culture must be developed to the extent that the workers are aware of the necessity of their revolutionary destiny. In practice, the success of the broad strategy depended upon the possibilities for making a general strike, the concerted withholding of wage labour designed to force a confrontation with capitalist economic and police power. Then, as today, reformist socialists believed the general strike to be a chimera, although its power was demonstrated in Russia in 1905 (and subsequently in England in 1926 and in France in 1968).

For Sorel the general strike never lost its validity as a serious weapon of the proletariat, but even he at times recognised that the political climate required a certain circumspection. He admitted that, because the idea of the general strike had become 'odious to the majority of socialist leaders' by 1897, he withheld a piece he had written on the subject, so as not to be dismissed by them out of hand. But in 1900 the tide rose again in the form of a new strike wave and he observed with pleasure that 'the general strike was no longer considered a simple anarchist insanity'.[15] He looked forward to the time when the general strike would become generally inseparable from the idea of proletarian revolution itself.

But what was, or is, the 'general strike'? Was it a tactic, a strategy or merely an event that some waited for eagerly and some with misgivings? Would socialists lead a general strike or would they be pushed by it? These were the questions which called for a critical examination of socialist practice and it is not hard to understand why the parliamentary socialists wished to ignore them. Sorel attempted to clarify these counter-tendencies by setting out 'three important facets' of the 'thesis' of the general strike.

The first thing that must be kept in mind is that to endorse the idea of a general strike is to express an essentially proletarian rejection of parliamentary politics. It in fact asserts that 'the era of political revolution' has been passed, at least in terms of its being of any possible benefit to the proletariat. In fact, the general strike represents a conscious rejection of the premises of capitalist political life. It is a declaration of the proletariat's refusal to take part in the hierarchical political system and the political ideology that allows capitalist management of social conflicts. To accept the general strike as the ultimate revolutionary weapon is to break with capitalist 'civility'. It is to cease to be humble in the face of the declaration of the rights of man, the idea of impartial justice for all, political constitutions and parliaments. It is to recognise that these institutions exist in their present forms in order to maintain the power of a certain social class. But it *does not* mean that to accept the idea of the general strike is to reject actual human freedoms or conscious communal organisation. Sorel maintained that, at base, the general strike involved not only the rejection of bourgeois government, but also of all hierarchies which more or less approximated to the bourgeois political system. 'Advocates of the general strike wish to eliminate all the aspects of bourgeois liberalism: demagoguery, the manipulation of public opinion, party alliances.'[16] If the proletariat understood that its interests could best be advanced by itself, using the power it had – the central role it plays in the productive process – political machinations and compromises

80

could not possibly be considered necessary or even effectual in the revolutionary process.

Thus Sorel's second 'facet' of the general strike has to do with the fact that it is a *concrete* method of fighting capitalism, whereas parliamentary politics is a means of deliberating with and dealing with capitalism. This facet is virtually inseparable from the third, which asserts that the general strike is not an *idea* born out of reflections on the philosophy of history; it is rather rooted in the actual practical experience of the proletariat. The revolutionary general strike will, in fact, represent the culmination of proletarian experiences as the working classes defend themselves on a day-to-day basis. It will represent a going-over to the offensive. Strikes by themselves will remain nothing but economic incidents if their revolutionary potentiality is not brought out by revolutionary workers. 'Each strike', Sorel maintained, 'no matter how local it may be, is a skirmish in the great confrontation that is called the general strike.' However, Sorel's terminology must not be taken too literally here. He did not wish to say that striking workers will necessarily learn actual combat techniques. But they *would* gain an even clearer understanding of their social position within the productive system. 'The practice of strikes' most importantly encourages 'a very clear conception of the class struggle.'[17]

These statements have a certain outmoded ring about them today. Since Sorel's time we have seen how strike activity can actually result in a dimmer view of the class struggle. Either defeat at the hands of a brutal alliance between industry and government, or a seeming victory, thanks to the conjecture of favourable conditions or an 'enlightened' capitalist management, can easily trim the critical edge of objective understanding from class awareness. Clearly, merely engaging in strikes will not lead automatically to a revolutionary class awareness. On the other hand, and as a marxist, Sorel was right to insist on the priority of direct working-class action. Putting aside the question of revolutionary 'leadership' for the moment, all marxists, whether they be of a 'leninist' or a 'libertarian' orientation, must ultimately conclude that in the end it is the proletariat itself that will 'make' a socialist revolution. And, in the light of this presumption, it remains legitimate to consider the strike as a microcosm of

81

revolution or as a school for revolution. It is also true, however, that the level of consciousness attained in that microcosm or in that school will depend upon both the individual efforts and the collective strength of the combatants. At any rate, as a marxist and as a revolutionary, Sorel was correct in saying that the importance of the strike in terms of working-class consciousness is the sense of solidarity to be gained from it. 'Marx expressed this fact well in saying that [working-class] coalitions have the result of eliminating competition between the workers' themselves.[18] This is an understanding that cannot be easily contested and it was and is still worth insisting upon when we consider that workers are constantly encouraged to delegate whatever natural authority they posssess to either politicians or union officials.

The question of strikes and their relation to the elevation of proletarian consciousness is central to the revolutionary process. For revolutionaries, strikes represent the best situations in which consciousness can be raised. For counter-revolutionaries, strikes are the premier test of the socio-political system's ability to defuse social conflicts – to co-opt working-class leadership and to make revolution seem nothing but a utopian fantasy. Sorel was early in recognising that the greatest danger facing the revolutionary movement, as far as strikes were concerned, was not the brutal repression that occurred from time to time, but rather the misleading sense of victory that could develop from 'managed' victories.

> Experience has shown that today it is much more difficult to restore economic order by frightening the workers by measures of repression, than it is by suggesting conciliatory solutions to the bosses, who are generally quite ignorant of their rights, conditioned to respect humbly representatives of the state, and almost always as timid as rabbits. And once the public has come to believe that the proletarian masses are invincible and that the bosses (through their weakness) must shoulder the responsibility for whatever inconveniences work stoppages impose on the country, it demands that the government intervene with all its power in order to force the heads of industry to make concessions to their workers.[19]

82

Although the strike was a very modern phenomenon in Sorel's day, the state had quickly stepped in to regulate conflicts and thus greatly complicated the practical, juridical and psychological content of what began as stark collisions between Capital and Labour.

The formal right to strike in France had existed only since the enactment of the law of 25 March 1864 which legalised labour coalitions. In France, as in all the industrial capitalist countries, it took some time before the state was able to 'catch up' with its own legislation. That is, having legalised the right to strike, the state was then obliged to devise ways of curtailing, managing and diverting strike activity. This problem was of course at the very core of all capitalist law: the gap between principle and practice which allows the coexistence of a universal system of formal legal equality and a social reality typified by social caste divisions, extreme economic inequality and the constant threat of political repression. Sorel accordingly drew a distinction between what he called 'strict law', and the 'halo' of the law – the 'halo' being all the grey areas which allow capitalist interests to be consciously served while ostensibly preserving the appearance of judicial non-partiality. It is for this reason, he believed, that lawyers would emerge (and have since emerged) as the most important professional group in the capitalist polity. Lawyers are generally much more capable, it being their job, than philosophers, economists or historians of understanding the content of a strike. Sorel observed that in his day there were some law professors who had 'enough intelligence, knowledge and courage to explain the truth about class struggle in their courses'. The young people who took these courses would, he predicted, occupy more important positions than their peers in the arts and sciences. 'They will be the directors of bourgeois consciousness. It will be through the work of its lawyers that the bourgeoisie will learn how the workers are being formed by socialism.'[20] And it is the lawyers who will assist the bourgeois state in its reaction to the growing collective power of the proletariat.

Sorel emphasised that the *apparent* successes of the organised workers could easily play into the hands of capitalist ideologists. When, for example, workers return to work after a more or less successful strike, which in formal or informal ways has involved the arbitration of the state, they are convinced that it was only because of their collective power that they won concessions (which, in the largest sense is of course true). However, due to a lack of objective perspective, workers often fail to understand 'the requirement of bourgeois order' which leads that state to arbitrate instead of simply repressing the strike.

In addition to the perhaps natural illusions which are created by state arbitration, new elements of capitalist ideological defence have emerged as a result of the labour movement. The notion of the 'right to work', for example, has entered into juridical consciousness. And while workers find it more than difficult to bring individual grievances to court, 'the administrative powers feel the need to act as if the collective mass of workers possessed the right to work. Thus strikes have given birth to the conception of the right to work as a part of common law.'[21] In this sense the collective rights of workers are recognised and a major part of the old *laissez faire* capitalist ideology has been discarded, thus moving the social relations of capitalist production and their corresponding politics into a new phase of development. The savage exploitation and repression of labour, which characterised and was necessary for the initial capital formation of large scale industry, must now give way before the need to come to terms with a more aware and powerful working-class population. The imperative of capitalist polity, therefore, is to counteract the effects of its own operation – to de-solidarise and to contain the social forces unleashed by its own dynamic. It will be necessary for the state to intervene in capital-labour relations in such a way that organised labour will become institutionalised. Working-class organisation must not be opposed so much as *absorbed* into the functional processes of both political and economic production.

The imperative of the revolutionary movement will be to resist this process of institutionalisation and, equally, to preserve the cultural and political autonomy of proletarian existence. Revolutionary workers must adapt to the changing circumstances by developing their own counter-institutions through conscious practice; and strikes are both a means of cultural defence and a strategy of social combat, of offence. The 'nature' of individual strikes will be the test of revolutionary awareness and *élan*. A

84

strike must be powered by a view of long-range revolutionary ends, the need to preserve and extend a sense of proletarian communality in the face of state integrationism and the necessity of revealing the essential incompatibility of proletarian and capitalist interests.

The morality of a strike must be rigid. 'In order to impair the workings of industry, strikers must establish their own police force, influence the general population with demonstrations and isolate authorities and comrades who are in opposition.' Thus the devising of its own mode of discipline and juridical thinking is a requirement for making a strike. But this must be done by the workers themselves; it will never happen if they follow demagogues who fill them with rhetoric about the justice of the popular cause. 'In order for the proletariat to acquire the idea of its revolutionary mission, it must have the ambition to create a juridical system' of its own. And if this is done, if the hopes and instincts of the proletariat are thus elaborated as a body of proletarian law and morality, 'a comparison of this system of proletarian justice with the bourgeois system would give a perfectly clear idea of the meaning of revolution'.[22] Strikes must therefore be carried out with the development of revolutionary class consciousness as their primary objective. For this reason the existence of a broad, loosely co-ordinated network of working-class organisations must exist in order to provide the sense of solidarity and collective power necessary to sustain militancy and a revolutionary perspective.

But such action should not be carried out with the idea that the proletariat must ignore the political workings of the capitalist system. To believe that the proletariat could develop into a revolutionary force by avoiding the reality of bourgeois political life would be a utopian error of the worst proportions. Without falling into reformism or a sort of 'revolutionary gradualism', the revolutionary syndicalist movement should nevertheless exploit every opportunity to split, divide and subvert the ruling power structure.

It is necessary that the *syndicats* expropriate these powers by demanding them without ceasing, by interesting the public in their efforts, by denouncing the abuses, and by

85

exposing the incapacity or dishonesty of the public administration. In doing this they will preserve what is good in the old system of bourgeois democracy and evade the traps and repression which are part of it. Thus a society will have been created with completely new elements and in accord with purely proletarian principles. The groups will have finished by extending their field of action so much that they will have absorbed almost all politics.

This is how, in the light of the materialist conception of history, I understand the definitive struggle for public power. It is not a struggle for positions occupied by the bourgeoisie or to share in their spoils; it is a struggle designed to empty the bourgeois political organism of all life, and to put whatever was useful in it into a proletarian polity which has developed along with the proletariat itself.[23]

Thus revolutionary syndicalism, far from being apolitical as its socialist critics maintained, was the *ultimate* politics when considered from a marxist perspective.

Revolutionary syndicalism transcended the capitalist mode of interest articulation by recognising the fundamental historical importance of 'objective' class struggle. Only conflict between the proletariat and the controllers of capital can move society towards a more rational balance between individual and communal interests. Socialist political parties have their role to play in the revolutionary process, Sorel was quick to acknowledge, but the class struggle must not be subordinated to electoral strategy. If it were, then the whole revolutionary movement would be rapidly transformed into a component part of the capitalist polity, subject to all the complicity, compromises, corruption and dishonesty endemic to capitalist psychology and culture. To attempt to lead the proletariat with grandly proclaimed promises of a fundamental change in their lives and social relations through the casting of a ballot, was to expose them to alternating bouts of expectation and disappointment which could only lead to apathy, depression and, perhaps, to radical conservatism.

The road to revolution engineered by Sorel was not particularly easy, but in its broad design it was in line with Marx's original conception of proletarian revolution. Only a progressive development of the proletariat's collective understanding of the incompatibility of their interests with the continuance of the capitalist mode of production could lead to social revolution. The *syndicats* would be the vehicles through which this understanding was developed and focused, and with which a sufficient measure of co-ordinated activity would be achieved. The proletariat needs leaders far less than it needs a positive understanding of its class-cultural uniqueness and its collective strength.

5. Embourgeoisement: The Politics of Culture in the Era of Monopoly Capitalism

Sorel's focus upon proletarian culture has proved to be the most important dimension of his work. Although he has been considered a 'moralist' because of the stress he put on 'the ethical and juridical' development of proletarian consciousness, the failure of the capitalist system to disintegrate quickly, both economically and socially, as Marx and most of the first marxists anticipated that it would, gives Sorel's observations a certain prophetic weight. He posed the problem starkly: the key to marxist analysis and to proletarian revolution was the unfolding of *conscious* class struggle. Each social class possessed a culture of its own which at its core was composed of moral precepts and ethical principles. It was only by becoming self-conscious of this cultural identity, and by realising why the thinking and behaviour of the proletariat was essentially different from that of the bourgeoisie, that the workers would understand the necessity of eliminating the productive system which produces the class structure and the culture of capitalist society.

Thus the question was usually posed, and for many it seemed to be posed too generally. For contemporary marxists, however, the problem of class culture cannot be easily dismissed. The role of class culture and of the political ideology within it often looms as *the* outstanding problem of revolutionary praxis. In the United States, for example, the development of both a sociology and a politics based upon the trend towards ideological 'consensus' and the imagined disappearance of separate class cultures has profoundly discouraged the 'old left' and has just as profoundly confused the 'new left'. The most powerful industrial-capitalist nation in the world possesses a proletariat with perhaps the least political class consciousness. Obviously it has been a combination of a relatively high standard of living and periodic repression that has weakened the working-class movement in the

88

United States. But what is to happen if the economic situation is aggravated to the point where social conflicts break out spontaneously once again? In the absence of a developed proletarian consciousness of its cultural uniqueness in relation to that of the capitalist classes, workers will lack the political clarity necessary to carry out and consolidate anything approximating to a proletarian revolution. From this perspective, the ideological assault made by the capitalist classes on the culture of the working classes should be considered the most serious facet of the class struggle.

In a broad sense, and from a marxist perspective, the recent interest in Gramsci's conception of the 'intellectual hegemony' of the ruling class is a new way of thinking about an old problem. After decades of attack upon class conceptualisation, welfare reformism, the suppression of revolutionary political organisations and the growing importance of bourgeois sociology as a vehicle of ideological transmission inside and outside the colleges, the notion of ideological hegemony is rather academic. Of more concrete interest are the means by which this 'hegemony' or, as the bourgeois sociologists came to call it, 'cultural integration' is achieved. Sorel observed the very beginnings of this process, when its effects did not go much beyond a certain opportunism that workers and socialists in general fell prey to. Nevertheless, given that the formation of a revolutionary proletarian class consciousness was the essential work of the socialist movement, Sorel believed that efforts to integrate workers culturally into bourgeois society were the greatest threat to the revolutionary movement. Thus, his mature writings revealed much concern for the phenomenon he called 'embourgeoisement': the assimilation, by the working classes, of bourgeois norms, ideas and modes of behaviour.

It should be noted that while the sociological expression 'cultural integration' refers to a process of assimilation, that of embourgeoisement expresses the content of that process. The idea was not that workers actually became or could become bourgeois in socio-economic terms, it meant rather that working people were capable of imitating bourgeois behaviour and adopting bourgeois values. The extent to which this imitative or inculcative process had actually occurred on a class basis remained

89

unclear in Sorel's work; and his lack of concreteness in this area is probably due to the fact that his assessment of embourgeoisement was conditioned by his hopes and fears.

In fact, the idea of embourgeoisement could be embarrassing for those who professed socialism, because it forced a confrontation between fundamental theoretical precepts and the degree to which those precepts conformed to political practice. Was it realistic for example, to regard society as made up of 'classes' with irreconcilably antagonistic interests dividing them? The question is intimately involved with the idea of 'class' itself. Certainly the 'class struggle' could not be discussed unless the notion of class had been thoroughly explored in relation to existing social divisions and relations. A political programme designed to achieve social revolution or the emancipation of the working class, if it were to succeed, could not merely restate formulas derived from the past as did the 'orthodox' Marxists. Nor could it simply be unconcerned with the relationship between theory and practice as the socialist reformers generally were.

If political action is designed to articulate and achieve social goals, then it must be founded upon an accurate understanding of society. Political action must be constantly invigorated by analysis, just as analysis should be continually enriched by practical action. It is now clear that over-optimism about the imminence of a proletarian revolution was a mistake in pre World War One France, especially when such optimism contributed to complacency or tactical blunders. Sorel was undoubtedly correct when he warned that the reformist rejection of class based political action would contribute to the weakness of the socialist and working-class movements. For him, it was just this relationship between the breakdown of revolutionary theory and the shifting contours of social relations and political consciousness that provided him with the inspiration to explore the imperatives of revolution in a changing society.

Sorel referred to Karl Kautsky as one who had already said much about these problems; and Bernstein, as we have seen, perhaps most clearly revealed the urgency of tactical questions to Sorel. It was Lenin who would eventually clarify the phenomenon of embourgeoisement by explaining in 1915 (in *Imperialism: The*

90

Highest Stage of Capitalism) that the condition was characteristic of capitalist society in its advanced phase of development.[1]

There is an apparent contradiction, perhaps a necessary one, in Sorel's various discussions of embourgeoisement. On the one hand, he saw it primarily as a psychological process, as the assimilation by the proletariat of bourgeois values, behavioural norms and self-concepts. On the other hand, his discussion of changing psychology, or psychology which had the potential for change, was coupled with an emphasis on the emergence of new social groups in France and on the complexity of the social structure in general. The cause of embourgeoisement was also ambiguous. Was it the result of propaganda, demagoguery and conditioning in the schools, or was embourgeoisement the consequence of higher earnings and a more elaborate division of labour? These are questions that Sorel did not attempt to answer completely. Perhaps it would be more accurate to say that he could not answer them completely. It is likely, however, that Sorel's emphasis on one or the other of these casual explanations depended in part upon his immediate perception of current events and the degree of optimism (or pessimism) he held concerning their outcome.

Sorel's ideas concerning embourgeoisement were most clearly expressed in the years between the beginning of the Dreyfus Affair and the merging of the socialist parties in 1905. However, although during this period he used the expression 'embourgeoisement' more frequently than at any other time, nothing emerged from his discussions that was sharply defined or systematised enough to be considered a theory. Sorel was more concerned with the practical problems of socialist tactics than with a need for rationally conceived systems.

Because the formation of proletarian class consciousness was, for Sorel, the 'alpha and omega' of socialism, the discussion of the antithetical process – embourgeoisement – must begin with the notion of 'class'. The idea of 'class', – essential to both socialist theory and revolutionary tactics – was endangered on two fronts. In the first place, it was under direct assault by the theorists and propagandists of bourgeois democracy. In the second place, the idea of class was being eaten away from within by the parliamentary socialists.

The requirements of parliamentary politics seemed to cause a certain rejection of the class struggle as an explanation of social processes and politics. After the early 1890s when the various socialist parties entered electoral politics with increasing success, Sorel perceived that the conceptual waters were becoming muddy in direct proportion to this electoral success. It was probably this concern that caused him to publish Karl Kautsky's article 'Socialism and the Liberal Professions' in the second number of *Le Devenir social* in 1895. This article (which appeared simultaneously in *Die Neue Zeit*) was primarily concerned with the increasing importance of the liberal professions and their effect on the socialist movement. Capitalist society, Kautsky said, was not made up of two homogeneous factions – the bourgeoisie and the proletariat. It was of a more complex and shifting composition. Society was in a perpetual state of transformation as new social groups were created in accordance with the needs of a developing productive system. The class struggle was certainly a valid and 'fundamental proposition'; but it must be only a starting point, because the relationships between the bourgeoisie and the proletariat change as social conditions change.

This changing state of social relations is reflected in the changing status and behaviour of social groups which are seemingly 'between' the bourgeoisie and the proletariat. These intermediate 'strata' have particular interests which change rapidly, allying them sometimes with the proletariat and sometimes with the bourgeoisie. The important thing is that, just as the political power, goals and tactics of these intermediate strata change naturally in accordance with social conditions, so the socialist movement must be aware of these developments and take account of them. 'The task of socialist theoreticians is to study these changes and to inform the militants of them.'[2]

In November of the same year that Kautsky's article appeared in *Le Devenir social*, Sorel took issue with the notion that society is nothing but two monolithic armies engaged in mortal combat: 'One has a very false idea of modern society when one reduces everything to a struggle between two armies ranged in battle; things are not as simple as that, and even in England the struggle does not have such a character.'[3] This was not to say that a struggle did not exist. The struggle existed everywhere and in many forms; but the problem was how to recognise the immediate nature of the struggle so as to be better able to sharpen it. This required a more subtle consideration of social developments and political forces. By 1897, Sorel had harped on the issue so much that it had affected his relationship with Paul Lafargue. In December 1897 he wrote to Croce that 'Lafargue has almost excommunicated me for having stated some doubts about the division of classes'.[4]

By 1901 Sorel was even more struck by the importance of these 'intermediate' social strata. In Charles Peguy's journal, *Les Cahiers de la Quinzaine*, he indicated a dual development which he thought would adversely affect proletarian consciousness. While the transformation of capitalism was producing a 'great variety of social strata', the existence of which tended to 'erase traditional lines of vocational demarcation', simultaneously the coalescence of organised political parties was characterised by an effort 'to dissimulate material interests under ideological aspects'.[5] Thus by 1901 Sorel was even more concerned with the problem, since it would obviously take more than a mere refinement of socialist theory to invigorate the socialist movement. The assertive self-confidence displayed by the Dreyfusards, and particularly by the politically aggressive university professors, increased his fear that working-class consciousness was perhaps as likely to become less revolutionary as to become more so. When his *Reflections on Violence* appeared in 1908 Sorel was writing to save the very notion of social class from those 'dissimulating' efforts of the bourgeois sociologists.[6]

The emergence of a truly revolutionary class consciousness has often been paralleled in the minds of 'orthodox' or vulgar marxists with the decline of religious belief, or conversely, with the rise of secularism. While this may be valid on the 'macro' historical level, it makes less sense as a basis for action in the maelstrom of immediate political events. This was a particularly confusing problem in France before World War One because of the debate over the relation between church and state in general, and over clerical education in particular. If increased secularisation were a positive gain in the work of raising working-class consciousness, what position should the socialist revolutionary

93

take when faced with an aggressive reformist effort to weaken the power of the church over the people and form a strong bourgeois political party in the process?

For Sorel the church was a less powerful and dangerous enemy than the bourgeoisie, which would assume whatever authority the church vacated as a result of this 'reformist' effort. In the modern world, christian education did not inspire the credulity it had generated in former times. However, the 'moral' and 'civic' education advocated by the bourgeoisie – in tones of increasing insistence – was more than relevant to the structural imperatives of industrial France, and thus capable of modifying working-class consciousness and behaviour in a durable fashion. So, for Sorel, the central problem of socialist political action was the raising of a militant class consciousness in the working class before the bourgeois reformers could effectively retard that development.

But first Sorel had to identify the problem as one involving bourgeois co-option of working-class consciousness. Actual tendencies were not as clear in 1895 as they would be after the Dreyfus Affair, but Sorel was already beginning to sort things out, largely in response to the actions of the parliamentary socialists. The appearance of a significant working-class movement in the early 1890s had intensified a trend towards state intervention in the economy and social affairs, which was at bottom a class response. It was the frightened response of 'the diverse factions of the class menaced by the proletarian revolution' who had come to understand that it is necessary to prepare institutions in advance if they were not to be swamped in the revolutionary tide. In other words, the irrationality of a *laissez faire* political economy must be reduced in the interests of a stable political environment. Although the objective conditions were historically unprecedented, the form of this class response was nothing new. Most simply, Sorel explained, 'capitalism has decided to buy peace at the necessary price' – something it had always done when its vital interests were threatened. Thus there were 'provident societies, consumer co-operatives run by discount capitalists, insurance plans, etc.' – all attempts at co-option of the workers in Sorel's estimation. Sorel did not see these attempts as the work of bourgeois evil geniuses, but rather as a completely logical class response to new imperatives of capitalist social order: 'Their plan does not require much imagination, because our adversaries limit themselves to taking up the old idea of the necessity for "social continuity".' The bourgeoisie had often sought either to 'create an intermediary class' or conversely 'to disorganise the proletariat by creating in its midst interests in apparent contradiction with those of the working class'.[7]

This last statement is perhaps the key to Sorel's fears regarding the state of working-class consciousness. The objective of the bourgeoisie was in part the construction of a façade of 'apparent' social change which the working class would accept and ultimately defend as they would defend themselves, leaving the bourgeoisie its social and political dominance through its possession and control of the capitalist economy. More important, even if economic developments were to create a revolutionary situation, the formation of revolutionary class consciousness would be more difficult because working-class psychology would have become seriously malformed through its contact with – and assimilation of – the bourgeois mentality. Sorel was thus faced with a new tactical problem. Not only was it necessary to educate the workers about theory and practice, but it was also increasingly necessary to undermine and expose the class bias of bourgeois reasoning directly before it seriously infected the working class with counter-revolutionary values and thought patterns.

There was not much time to waste in 1905: 'For a number of years the people who wish to realise social peace have sought to lead as many intelligent and active workers as they can to this petty-bourgeois spirit, because they know it is a sure way to neutralise them.'[8] This was Sorel's reason for writing *Illusions of Progress*, which appeared in 1908. The book was an attempt, using the 'historical methods of Marx', to study and expose bourgeois ideology.[9] It was a materialist critique of eighteenth-century rationalism and, by implication, the social reformism and sociology of his own day. It was an analysis of bourgeois justifications for liberal democracy which, while progressive in their pre-revolutionary historical context, were counter-revolutionary in an industrial-capitalist society.

'All our efforts', Sorel was saying, 'must help prevent bourgeois ideas from poisoning the rising class; this is why one cannot do enough to sever all links existing between the people and the literature of the eighteenth century.'[10] The 'illusions of progress' were those ideas promoting a sense of satisfaction or complacency regarding political and juridical innovations made during the French Revolution and after. Free enterprise and political democracy might be 'progress' for the bourgeoisie, but for the proletariat they represented capitalist exploitation.

There were, however, some groups in society that were all too ready to be 'poisoned' – workers who knowingly and eagerly aped the bourgeoisie. Generally, these people were the so-called 'aristocracy of labour', positive evidence to the bourgeoisie that democracy was working and equally positive evidence to Sorel that socialist tactics were not. The aristocracy of labour was the result, seemingly, of capitalism's benevolence. For those who had the necessary 'will', economic well-being lay in store, and with material prosperity would come social 'respectability'. All this was at hand if only the proletariat would accept capitalism as being essentially benevolent and uplift themselves and their families by working hard and thinking positively. This was the reasoning that Sorel strove to expose as false and which prompted him to oppose the principle of 'social continuity' so vigorously.

Who were these 'aristocrats' of the working class? In 1895 Sorel used the general expression 'petit-bourgeois' to describe them; but he also implied that these petty-bourgeois, or labour aristocrats, should properly be considered part of the proletariat. In fact, these people were an artificial 'class', considered in terms of direct productive relations, because they were dependent upon the state for their existence and well-being. If capitalists had decided to buy social peace, they had to buy people; and the aristocracy of labour were the ones who had sold out, perhaps not consciously, but who supported the state because of their condition of dependence on it.

In the 1890s Sorel was thinking primarily of workers whose immediate material interests were linked to the operation of state bureaucracies. Later on, he would expand his discussion and be more precise about these people, but for the moment he thought of them as a buffer class. He called it a 'plebe' which forms 'the army of mercenaries that capitalism opposes to the proletariat'. The development of the capitalist economy creates this army. As industry is consolidated, the number of unemployed workers increases and the state is forced to devise means of absorbing surplus labour, in pursuit of its overriding objective of maintaining social peace – of resolving social antagonisms. Thus it is that 'governments are obliged to augment the expenses of their budgets each year in very great proportions'.

This is an analysis similar to some recent explanations of the 'welfare state'; but Sorel went further than most, by tying his analysis directly into Marx's dialectical conception of the historical process. While the state is forced to expand its activities, because of the emergence and continued development of large scale industry, the state in turn encourages further consolidation of industry, thus producing greater regulatory problems and, ultimately, greater state control and authority. Part of the state's answer to the problem was to compound the problem. In order to control the working masses, industry must be rationalised by further consolidation. 'In order to maintain its plebeian clientele, the state has a strong tendency to create monopolies in which the unemployed workers, those rejected by industry, can be regimented.'[11] Sorel never took the next step of describing this process as a new 'stage' of capitalism as Lenin did, but many of the elements are there.

For Sorel, the existence of an aristocracy of labour did not mean that capitalism was changing itself for the better. It meant that new methods of exploitation and control were being devised. Far from being a justification of the reformist strategy, the presence of these 'aristocrats' dramatised the difficulty of the struggle against the bourgeoisie. What the proletariat faced was a new form of domination in capitalist society. And any apparent antagonism between the state and capital was deceptive because, while capitalism was now dependent upon the state, the state existed because of the political requirements of capitalism.

The symbiotic relationship between the state and capital was put into bold relief for Sorel by the ease with which *laissez faire* gave way to statism. 'The capitalist gives up his prerogatives to the state quite voluntarily', because he realises that it is in his interest to do so.[12] Not only will government labour legislation

97

create pacific social conditions and regulate the labour market more effectively, but the industrialist also has need of tariff protection and other state shields against international competition or overt aggressions. The essential point is that the emergence of statism and the emergence of a working-class aristocracy are different aspects of the same historical process – the transformation of capitalist production.

In terms of working-class consciousness the aristocracy of labour could be considered the perpetuation of a traditional attitude. The British working class, always the classic model because British capitalism had experienced the most intensive and extended development, offered the best 'bad example'. According to Sorel, the English workers were in the grip of a 'guild' mentality. One had only to study the English working-class movement briefly to understand that it had been 'distinguished by an extraordinary incomprehension of the class struggle'. Sorel did not indicate whether or not this was a case of retarded class consciousness or the blunting of a consciousness that once existed, but he placed much of the blame on the British trade unions and British reformism, noting that it was not for nothing that 'for England the expression "labour aristocracy" has been invented'.[13]

The existence of the aristocracy of labour posed difficulties for theoretical socialism mainly because it threatened the notion of class exclusiveness so dear to orthodox marxists. As it was, the doctrinal narrowness of Jules Guesde began to give way to Bernstein's explanation of old myths and new realities, paving the way for the acceptance of marxist revisionism. But although Bernstein's observations influenced Sorel as well, he rejected Bernstein's conclusions because they represented a reformist deviation away from marxist revolutionism whereas his formulations would be based upon 'what I will call the marxism of Marx', and remain revolutionary.[14] In Sorel's mind, a combination of real social developments, the state of working-class awareness, socialist politics, and the decomposition of theoretical marxism had combined to create a 'crisis of socialism'.

Perhaps the most insidious aspect of embourgeoisement, in Sorel's estimation, was that the leaders of the organised socialist parties were the principal carriers of it. Considered in this light,

the 'official socialists' were no different from bourgeois politicians. The socialists 'too often follow the example of the
radicals' in that 'they wish to make their clientele bourgeois,
and they only seem to be able to preach the imitation of the
upper classes'.[15] Following a reformist programme, the official
socialists encouraged the emulation of bourgeois culture and
thus affirmed the legitimacy of capitalist society. The official
socialists were actually validating a principle of bourgeois
social science, that of 'imitation', and helping to create
that 'social continuity' which, as a popular conception, has
the potential of being a main bulwark of industrial-capitalist
society.

There is a certain fatalism that permeates all of Sorel's
discussions of embourgeoisement. In his *Introduction to Modern
Economy* (1903), he indicated that modern industry, by destroying
the 'links which attach workers to their trade . . . increases their
susceptibility to bourgeois ideas', because of the indeterminacy
of new social relationships. If at first the bonds between the
workers and their craft are broken by the displacement of
artisanal work by industrial production, and then class divisions
are obscured by higher salaries and by ideological conditioning,
there would be a difficult task facing a revolutionary movement
founded ideologically upon the idea of a class struggle.

It is in this area that Sorel's observations might appear
analytically weakest, because it seems anachronistic to pin the
hope for an industrial proletarian revolution upon the juridical
conceptions of an artisanal working people. It appears, however,
that Sorel was stressing the importance of ethical-juridical
notions that were conducive to the class struggle (for example
conceptions of co-operation, communal solidarity, the 'just
price' for labour time, and the integral nature of the work
process) and to combine them with an understanding of modern
industrial conditions and social relationships, thus forming a
new synthesis of revolutionary theory and action. As Sorel saw it,
it was a singular dilemma that the French working class faced.
On the one hand there was the example of 'the embourgeoisement
of the English workers who imitate all the buffoonery of the upper
classes of their country'; and, on the other hand, 'efforts being
made today to "civilise" the working classes'.[16] Were the French

99

workers fated to share the experience of their English comrades, or could concerted and militant action, more informed because of the unfortunate British example, put the revolutionary process back upon the desired course with the requisite momentum? This was the question Sorel faced while complacency or opportunism reigned in French socialist circles.

Sorel's difficulty was to be aware of the prevailing constraints placed upon revolutionary praxis in a tantalising historical situation. Even though the reformist cadres of the bourgeoisie had launched a formidable ideological and institutional assault, was not revolutionary syndicalism gaining new recruits every day in the years before 1906? And it seemed that revolutionary sentiments were growing in the wake of the Russian Revolution of 1905. For a while after the Dreyfus Affair, particularly in the years 1905 and 1906, it looked as if revolution were imminent, especially if the outspoken fears of the defenders of bourgeois democracy were given any weight.

There is not much doubt that Sorel was encouraged by these developments, and in fact most of his writing from this period is markedly more optimistic. For example, in November 1905 he published an unusually optimistic article in which he claimed that the leaders of the socialist parties were like freshwater fish who had somehow found themselves in the ocean and who swam about without knowing where they were, where they were going, or how to take precautions against storms. The syndicalists, on the other hand, had true revolutionary zeal and perspective and had already 'raised the tone of the struggle' to the point where 'the instinct of war is reinforced in the same proportion as the bourgeoisie has made concessions to social peace'.[17] This article was much more a propaganda tract than a theoretical analysis, as Sorel's uncharacteristic use of the term 'war' to describe the class struggle indicates. And it is certainly one of the most optimistic and enthusiastic pieces Sorel ever wrote until the Bolshevik revolution. It was definitely a change from his thinking in July 1903 when he wrote to his friend Paul Delesalle that he feared the 'frightening work of embourgeoisement' being done in the *syndicats* which represented 'an enormous effort' by 'the friends of Jaurès'.[18] However, even in the more encouraging atmosphere of two years later, Sorel warned that 'syndicalism is menaced by the "bourgeoisme" of the large federations'.[19]

Sorel's pessimism caused him to study the problem of political consciousness thoroughly. His approach to the question was similar to that later developed by Herbert Marcuse, whose writings are also fatalistic and prone to dwell primarily upon the psychological obstructions barring the way to revolutionary consciousness. In fact, it was Marcuse who would eventually give new attention to a disturbing question which Sorel posed during a discussion held by the French Philosophy Society in April 1902. The topic was the significance of 'luxury' in modern society; and the single statement made by Sorel revealed how important he believed recent economic developments to be in terms of their influence upon modern mentalities. Sorel suggested that puritan restrictions on consumption were now irrelevant and increasingly disregarded, because the era of the primitive accumulation of capital was definitely over. 'Today', Sorel said, 'it is being said that the development of a certain luxury in the most numerous classes is a motor of their progress.' Although he did not elaborate the point, it is evident that Sorel had more than a premonition of another aspect of embourgeoisement – that in which the worker is considered to be more economically important as a 'consumer' than as a producer. Since France was not yet a full-blown 'consumer society' managed by a 'welfare state', it is perhaps understandable that Sorel was not able to develop this idea to greater lengths. So he was condemned to cry virtually alone in the French revolutionary wilderness and warn of the formation of a 'lower bourgeoisie' which would be used to support a highly centralised bureaucratic state and contribute to the destruction of revolutionary consciousness. He insisted all the while, however, that he could not 'accept the idea that the proletariat has the historical mission of imitating the bourgeoisie'.[20]

World War One, with its attendant chauvinism, sustained Sorel's fears about the state of proletarian consciousness and the socialist commitment to a revolutionary strategy. In August 1920 he wrote to Croce that 'the government can buy socialists like speculators buy cattle', and that 'the people, corrupted by high salaries, have become indifferent to everything'.[21] However, he was excited and enthusiastic about the Bolshevik revolution, which he supported wholeheartedly and regarded as brightening the long-term prospects for socialism all over the world, even if it should fail. Thus it appeared to Sorel that World War One had accelerated the process of embourgeoisement while simultaneously raising socialist hopes.

To face the problem of working-class culture in relation to that of the capitalist classes from a revolutionary perspective, is the most difficult task a marxist can assume. When Sorel attempted it, he was working pretty much in the dark, in the days when a much more limited body of revolutionary socialist theory was available, and when the socialist movement was much less compromised than it is now by collaboration with established powers. Whether or not higher salaries, ideological conditioning, statism, or the continuing division of labour and the emergence of new social strata was the principal cause of embourgeoisement, Sorel correctly asserted that the important consideration for a revolutionary movement must be to respond positively to new revolutionary imperatives.

If Sorel's principal contribution to marxism was his focus upon the importance of proletarian culture in its relation to revolutionary class consciousness, he has been most often portrayed as an irresponsible proponent of violence. Bourgeois writers tend to dismiss Sorel as an 'irrationalist' because he honestly addressed the question of the role of violence in the proletarian struggle.[22]

But Sorel's *Reflections on Violence* was far from being an 'anarchist cookbook'. In fact he did not advocate any precise mode of violent activity, limiting himself to embracing the 'collective' violence endemic to strikes as opposed to the non-constructive violence of individual terrorism.[23] In his conception, violence is any form of physical activity which tends to undermine the social order. 'Force', on the other hand, is any attempt of a governing minority to impose the organisation of the established social order.[24] We can imagine that Sorel had in mind the physical protection of strikes against scabbing and military and police aggressions, but, because he was not specific, we can only assume it.

Sorel's purpose was not to suggest a particular mode of

102

proletarian conduct, but rather to ratify the reality of militant strike activity. Such ratification was necessary because of firstly, the pervasive effects of bourgeois ideology and propaganda which claimed that all violence was a form of barbarity, opposed to right 'reason' and 'progress',[25] and secondly, the counter-revolutionary ministrations of parliamentary socialists, who did not wish to lose their positions as 'leaders' of the socialist movement in the eyes of the bourgeoisie.[26] On the broadest level, he believed that only a militant proletarian movement, unafraid of accepting the consequences of true class struggle, could keep class lines clear, hasten the revolution, and thus forestall the 'barbarism' which would result should the revolutionary movement be temporarily crushed and capitalist 'force' be allowed to reign unchecked.

Reflections on Violence was originally published in 1906 in the form of several articles, at a time when strike activity was particularly intense. Sorel had hopes that a general strike might develop if the workers were militant and confident enough; consequently he tried to increase their militancy by explaining the utility of a militant proletarian attitude which did not rule out violence. Over all, Sorel said much the same thing as Frantz Fanon was to develop in more detail (in *The Wretched of the Earth*) about the uplifting psychological effects of working class aggression.

The emergence of concerted efforts to integrate the French working class culturally into bourgeois society was such a major challenge to socialist theory and practice, that to ignore it was to sink into a state of doctrinaire impotence. The development of bourgeois sociology and reformism was not an isolated phenomenon or a harmless threat to the socialist movement; it was a rational response to class struggle that involved a compelling ideological justification for the pursuit of certain political interests. The principles of the new sociology were directly antithetical to the postulates of marxist socialism, at a time when marxism was just beginning to influence working-class consciousness. The determined effort to give the masses a 'moral' or 'civic' education based upon the formulations of the new sociology must be regarded as an all-out ideological assault upon

103

the problems created for bourgeois democracy by industrial upheaval and socialist propaganda. The question could not be ignored as Guesde in France and Kautsky in Germany chose to ignore it; nor could it be compromised with, as Jaurès in France and Bernstein in Germany chose to, by becoming the accomplices of anti-socialist reformers.

With his discussion of embourgeoisement, Sorel posed the question of 'false consciousness' raised by Marx in *The German Ideology*. How and why did individuals often share a world view which did not conform to their class interests? It was, and is, the most central and important question marxists can ask, for it involves the most basic task of revolutionaries: how to remove the obstacles in the way of the formation of revolutionary class consciousness. Only this work can create a revolutionary situation. Surely, through its own dynamic, the capitalist mode of production will produce socio-cultural alienation – an increasingly lifeless and frustrating spiritual void. On its own, the capitalist system will generate social conflicts and will devise new forms of repression. Its need for capital, sources of investment and increased production will cause an economic implosion – a collapsing towards the centre which will involve mounting economic misery and political violence. But there is no reason why the capitalist ruling class cannot maintain their control over this economic breakdown indefinitely.

The capitalist power structure has need only of loyal military and police forces, *plus* a population which does not have a clear understanding of its potential strength and capacity for humane social organisation. In the end, ideological control is the last defence of any oppressive polity. To destroy the prestige of upper-class culture, to undermine respect for political 'leaders,' to expose the lies and hypocrisy which mask ruling class interests and politics, this is the work which Sorel felt was proper for non-proletarian revolutionaries. Those who claimed to 'represent' proletarian interests by participating in bourgeois politics, maintaining the conventions of bourgeois culture, and seeing the class struggle as the struggle to win general acceptance of a more 'rational' distribution of capitalist wealth were false revolutionaries who must be denounced along with those who frankly professed faith in the capitalist system.

104

'Embourgeoisement' was a word with which Sorel described all forms of anti-proletarian thinking. For the proletariat and workers of all kinds, it could involve the mechanism of commodity fetishism, the influence of abstract 'rationalistic' education in the schools, the imitative 'need' for social status in a class-ordered society, the temptation of power in a competitive culture and the fear of non-conformity in an atmosphere of regimented 'individualism'. For the middle classes, embourgeoisement could encompass the fear of proletarianisation and the consequent obsession with maintaining social distance through aesthetic pretensions. It could be defined as the petty-bourgeois need to suppress social conflicts of all kinds – so disturbing are they to the limited social vision and political courage of those caught in the vice of class conflict, those 'in-between' the ruling class and the proletariat. In this way the concept of embourgeoisement expressed the cultural dimension of class struggle at every level of revolutionary combat.

After the publication of *Reflections on Violence* in 1908, Sorel became immensely more well-known, but it was not to his advantage. The inflammatory title of the book hid its real intention and isolated Sorel even more. In addition, the relative check of revolutionary syndicalism after several years of militant strike activity contributed to an atmosphere of defeat in the years preceding World War One.

Sorel began to break with those who had been his comrades. In 1909 he ceased to publish in *Le Mouvement socialiste*, an important revolutionary journal oriented towards revolutionary syndicalism, claiming that its chief editor, Hubert Lagardelle, was becoming reformist and opportunistic (and, in fact, Lagardelle later emerged as a supporter of French fascism). At the same time he stopped holding court at Charles Peguy's bookshop near the Sorbonne. He could not tolerate Peguy's growing mystic nationalism. In 1910 he attended the funeral of Paul and Laura Lafargue, victims of the general depression reigning in revolutionary circles (they committed suicide). Symbolically, and probably unknown to Sorel, Lenin was also at the Lafargues' graveside. The encounter marks well the transition to a new phase of the revolutionary movement, from the era of the Second International to the semi-clandestine strategies of 'vanguard' revolutionary organisations.

But if Sorel's allegiance to the strategy of revolutionary syndicalism ran counter to the idea of an elite, vanguard party of the proletariat staffed largely by intellectuals, he nevertheless reacted, as almost all revolutionaries did, with tremendous enthusiasm for the Bolshevik revolution. For example, he used the occasion of a re-publication of his *Reflections on Violence* to add an appendix – titled 'For Lenin', in which he responded to a claim that Lenin was influenced by the book. 'I haven't the least reason', he said, 'to imagine that Lenin has taken some ideas from my books; but if this has been the case, I would be more than proud to have contributed to the intellectual formation of a man whom I consider to be the greatest socialist theoretician since Marx and chief of state with a genius comparable to that of Peter the Great.'[27] Even if the 'plutocrats of the Entente' succeeded in crushing the Bolshevik revolution, he said, the ideology produced by the system of soviets would not perish. At the very least, 'the Russian workers are acquiring an immortal glory in approaching the realisation of what has been only an abstract idea'.[28]

Regardless of his belief in the necessity of proletarian autonomy, there is no evidence that Sorel opposed the formation of a potentially powerful French Communist Party after World War One. The C.G.T. was by that time, after all, ridden with opportunism. Sorel's intimate friend Paul Delesalle collaborated actively with the new party, and Sorel himself began to publish in the *Revue communiste*. He did so until his death in 1922; and Delesalle wrote Sorel's obituary for the communist newspaper *l'Humanité*.

During the last few years of his life, Sorel suffered poor health and poverty. He was forced to sell his cottage as a result of the war and the Russian revolution (his savings were invested in Austrian and Russian bonds!). But while his refusal of a state pension in 1892 caused him considerable material hardship, he remained, as he said of himself, 'a disinterested servant of the proletariat'. He retained, as well, his political and ideological independence. Although sick and poverty striken, he wrote for the

Revue communiste, the intellectual organ of red revolution; and in his will he requested that his coffin be covered with a black flag.

Epilogue

Sorel's marxism was distinguished by its relative lack of philosophical pretentiousness and its stress upon the role of ideology in social dynamics. If he wrote on a variety of esoteric topics in addition to his directly political writings, he remained un-'theoretical' in the sense that the direct analytical *application* of marxist principles can be seen in almost all his writings. For him, historical materialism was a new world view – a radically different way of perceiving social reality which carried with it a fundamental critique of capitalism. The work of marxists should be to analyse capitalist reality in such a way as to clarify it, to expose it to view, and to undermine its worth in the eyes of the proletariat. Thus, Sorel's approach remained essentially that of the engineer rather than that of the designer: he was less interested in formulating a 'theory' which could be considered a 'contribution' to marxism, than he was in contributing to the work of ideological negation that the revolutionary process must entail.

Nevertheless Sorel's work can be placed within a line of conceptual development. After all, the object of his analysis was a productive and political reality which was developing in accordance with its own dynamic. In France, his work represented a critical reaction to an emerging reformism. It was a warning to socialists that the capitalist state was changing its methods of social control, from paternalism and authoritarianism to co-option and ideological manipulation. In addition, it was a critique of reformist trends within the revolutionary movement. His criticism of the revolutionary 'party' – electoral or otherwise – as the central mode of revolutionary organisation, was in fact part of the proletarian movement which revolutionary syndicalism in France represented. This force – revolutionary syndicalism – was the most practical application of marxist principles. Yet it was to be effectively broken in all the capitalist countries, first by

108

the nationalist insanity whipped up during World War One, and then by the mystique of the revolutionary party inspired by the Bolshevik revolution and institutionalised everywhere by the new Communist Parties. Sorel's work was generally unacceptable to the authoritarian French Communist Party.

Sorel's marxism emerged from the generation which came between that of Marx and Engels and that of Lenin. He attempted to determine and then apply the essentials of Marx's conceptual breakthroughs in an historical context which was not yet coloured by the apparent success of what has come to be called leninism. In doing so he treated certain questions which have only gradually re-emerged as major foci of revolutionary attention. Embourgeoisement, especially, would emerge much later as a preoccupation for revolutionaries.

Lenin himself, for example, independently developed analyses similar to Sorel's of social and ideological trends in the industrial-capitalist countries. In the explanation of the failure of the Second International that Lenin worked out in his *Imperialism*, the creation of a privileged sector of the proletariat was succinctly described as a facet of capitalist development. Lenin too, like Sorel, chose the English experience as the best example. Monopoly capitalism has a special social and political dimension as well as a new mode of productive organisation. If the working class can be politically neutralised by splitting it into opposed privileged and non-privileged sectors at the cost of a relatively minor share of the profit, it is a small price to pay for social peace. To raise the general standard of living when productivity and profits are rising is only good political sense. Combine large doses of institutionalised propaganda (schools and communications media) with commodity fetishism and you will have the embourgeoisement of a significant part of the working class. For Sorel, for Lenin and for us today, the problem is the same – only its stage of evolution is different. Although a process of cultural homogenisation continues in the western capitalist world, a new cycle of proletarianisation and relative economic hardship is weakening the hold of embourgeoisement, thus posing again the question of proletarian politics.

After the Bolshevik revolution, the problem was resolved in marxist theory by the idea of the leninist vanguard party; and

109

revolutionary syndicalism ceased to have the appeal it once had. Antonio Gramsci's thinking on the matter reflects the impact of the Bolshevik revolution. While Sorel's observations about the phenomenon of embourgeoisement were the kind of evidence underlying Gramsci's conclusion that a major task of revolutionaries would be to counter the ideological hegemony of the ruling class, they saw the 'intellectuals' in a different light. To both, the importance of intellectuals to the revolutionary movement was obvious: they must use their literacy and their analysis, as Sorel said, to destroy the prestige of bourgeois culture. But whereas Sorel considered socialist intellectuals to be necessarily petty-bourgeois regardless of their origins, and thus removed from proletarian life and culture, Gramsci was influenced enough by the Bolshevik experience to reserve a leading role for intellectuals in the vanguard party. According to Sorel delegating this sort of authority to 'revolutionary intellectuals' (organic or not) opens the way for the intrusion into the proletarian movement of such petty-bourgeois attitudes as intellectual arrogance and authoritarianism. Only in recent years has revolutionary syndicalism begun to regain its attractiveness as an alternative to political party organisation. The long-term self-discrediting of the stalinist and post-stalinist Soviet Union and the Communist Parties of western Europe and the United States has played its role. A kind of 'crisis of authoritarianism' has overtaken revolutionary politics in the west.

But the tendency to reject traditional party organisation, 'democratic centralism' included, does not at all mean that one must turn to the simplistic anarchist utopianism of the past. What is needed, rather, is the liberation of marxist analysis from the straitjacket of authoritarian dogma. For too long now, marxism has been identified in the popular mind with the Soviet Union and the countries of eastern Europe, or with the various Communist Parties. Now the cycle of repression is breaking under its own weight and a true revolutionary marxism, a marxism of proletarian revolution, is emerging beyond the confines of the trotskyist parties and isolated libertarian marxist groups which have struggled against bureaucratic authoritarianism over the last few decades.

But this new phase of marxist revolutionism has not been a
110

painless birth. In reacting against the old dogmatic models of socialist organisation and ideology, the so-called 'New Left' precipitously adopted new models, particularly those from Latin America and the non-western world in general. The almost military maoist model of revolution, the rural-based dynamics of Latin-American revolution as outlined in Régis Debray's *Revolution in the Revolution?* and – in the United States – the tendency to follow the example of the movement for black liberation, were all aspects of a single collective attempt to find an alternative course of revolutionary struggle. In the 1970s, these trends gradually gave way to the re-emergence of an almost classical revolutionary sectarianism, as the New Left immersed itself in marxist theory. Yet, whatever the outward form of this process of ideological transformation, at base it represented a gradual rediscovery of the proletariat; for the New Left movement was largely a petty-bourgeois, radical movement which, when not rejecting the working class entirely, regarded it as having lost its revolutionary potential. Only the progressive assimilation of marxist philosophy and analysis gave the new generation of revolutionaries a deeper understanding of the historical dynamics of class struggle in general and the essential revolutionary role of the proletariat in particular. Of course this process is in no way merely one of ideas. The rapid proletarianisation of the relatively well-educated and affluent workers of the post World War Two generation has brusquely elevated working-class politics to a new level in the capitalist west.

Sorel's belief in revolutionary syndicalism as the most legitimate realisation of a marxist revolutionary strategy is shared by an increasing number of people. Not only did the French general strike of 1968 reveal the tremendous power possessed by the proletariat, but the incapacity of the leftwing political parties to contribute to the struggle was a further impetus to independent action. The fact is that the most important recent developments within the proletariat have taken place independent of political parties or existing labour organisations. Most outstandingly, the wave of factory occupations in western Europe since the early 1970s has demonstrated that when objective economic conditions are severe enough, workers instinctively protect their interests by simply seizing the means of production. Up to this point, marxism

111

is not particularly necessary for the working class; but to go beyond it – to take the offensive – the proletariat must have an understanding of how and why it is exploited and what can be done to end this exploitation. Most importantly, the proletariat must have confidence in its ability to finish with capitalist production. Remaining under the control or tutelage of union organisation or political parties can only produce confusion, slavishness and apathy. For this reason, Sorel's formulation of what marxism *should* be has gained more and more appeal in an era of mounting proletarian initiative and declining interest in authoritarian structures. Only a living, flexible revolutionary perspective and analysis will be creative enough to combat capitalism and create a foundation for socialism.

References

1. The Situation of Georges Sorel / pp.4-18

1. Georges Sorel, 'L'Ancien et la nouvelle métaphysique', *L'Ère nouvelle*, 1894, p.329.

2. Georges Sorel, 'Superstition socialiste?' *Le Devenir Social*, November 1895, p.733.

3. *Ibid*. p.745.

4. *Ibid*. p.748.

5. Antonio Gramsci, *Gramsci dans le texte*, Paris 1975, p.296.

6. In the first category are found the theses of professors Richard Humphrey (*Georges Sorel, Prophet without Honor*, Harvard 1951), James Meisel (*The Genesis of Georges Sorel*, Ann Arbor 1951), and Douglas Parnee (*Georges Sorel, a Reconsideration*, Cambridge 1952); and in the second category are works such as those of Irving Horowitz (*Radicalism and the Revolt against Reason*, London 1961), H. Stuart Hughes, (*Consciousness and Society*, London 1967), and Michael Curtis, (*Three against the Third Republic: Sorel, Barres and Maurras*, Princeton 1959).

7. Daniel Lindenberg, *Le Marxisme introuvable*, Paris 1975, p.7.

8. Jacques Julliard, *Fernand Pelloutier et les origines du syndicalisme d'action directe*, Paris 1971, p.194.

9. For example, the third of Sorel's works to be translated into English, *The Illusions of Progress*, appeared in 1969 (the second was *The Decomposition of Marxism*, which appeared as an appendix to Horowitz, *op. cit.*). In 1975 a large number of selected translations was published by Oxford Press, along with a serious introduction by John Stanley, a non-marxist who repeats some of the standard misconceptions, but who generally avoids caricaturing Sorel's thought.

10. Curtis, *op. cit.* p.51.

11. Jack Roth, 'The Roots of Italian Fascism: Sorel and Sorelismo', *Journal of Modern History*, 39, 1967, pp.42-43.

12. *Ibid*. p.40.

13. Herbert Marcuse, *Studies in Critical Philosophy*, London, New Left Books, 1972, p.149.

14. Jean-Paul Sartre, preface to Frantz Fanon, *The Wretched of the Earth*, Harmondsworth, Penguin 1967, p.12.

15. Julliard, *op. cit.* p.162.

16. See Harvey Goldberg, *Jean Jaurès*, Madison, Wisconsin 1962.

2. Marxism and Bourgeois Sociology: The Analytical Poles of Class Conflict / pp.19-42

1. Georges Sorel, 'La Position du problème de M. Lombroso', *La Revue scientifique*, Vol.51(7), 18 Feb. 1893, pp.206-9.

2. Georges Sorel, 'Le Crime politique', *La Revue scientifique*, Vol.51(18), 6 May 1893, p.561.

3. The idea that 'very diverse manifestations can be produced on the same base', he said, 'is one of the most important results of contemporary research'. Georges Sorel, 'La Femme criminelle', *La Revue scientifique*, Vol.52(15), 7 Oct. 1893, p.464.

4. Georges Sorel, 'Théories pénales de M. Durkheim et Tarde', *Archivio di Psichiatria, Scienze Penali ed Antropologia*, Vol.16(1895), p.224.

5. Georges Sorel, 'Les Théories de M. Durkheim', *Le Devenir social*, Vol.1(1), April 1895, p.16.

6. *Ibid.* p.156.

7. *Ibid.* p.150.

8. *Ibid.* p.24.

9. *Ibid.* p.2.

10. Georges Sorel, 'Les Fondements scientifiques de l'atomisme', *Annales de Philosophie chrétienne*, Vol.25(6), March 1892.

11. Georges Sorel, 'Les Fondements scientifiques de l'atomisme', *Annales de philosophie chrétienne*, Vol.26(1), April 1892, p.20.

12. Georges Sorel, 'Deux nouveaux sophismes sur le temps', *Annales de philosophie chrétienne*, Vol.26(4) Jan. 1892.

13. Franz Reuleaux, *Cinématiques, principes fondamentaux d'une théorie générale des machines*, Paris 1877, p.30.

14. *Ibid.* p.60.

15. *Ibid.* p.558.

16. *Ibid.* pp.555-56.

17. *Ibid.* pp.548-49.

18. See, for example, John L. Stanley's introduction to *From Georges Sorel*, John L. Stanley (ed.) New York 1976.

19. Pierre-Joseph Proudhon, *De la capacité politique des classes ouvrières*, Paris 1865, pp.53-54.

20. 'Lettres de Georges Sorel à Benedetto Croce, 1895-1922', *La Critica*, Vol.25, 1927.

21. Georges Sorel, preface to Antonio Labriola, *Socialism and Philosophy*, 3rd. edition, Chicago 1906, p.186.

22. Georges Sorel 'Le Matérialisme historique', séance du 20 mars 1902, *Bulletin de la Société Française de philosphie*, Vol.2, 1902. The following quotations are from pp.94-112.

3. The Politics of Class Struggle: Against the Reproduction of Capitalist Polity / pp.43-63

1. See V.I. Lenin, *Imperialism, The Highest Stage of Capitalism*, Moscow, Progress, 1966.

2. Georges Sorel, review of 'Waldeck-Rousseau, R. *Le Testament de Waldeck-Rousseau*', Paris 1904, in *Revue générale de bibliographie Française*, Vol.2, Jan 1904, p.555

3. Georges Sorel, 'Nouveaux réquisitoires de M. Brunetière', *Études socialistes,* Vol.1(3), May-June 1903, p.151.

4. See John McManners, *Church and State in France, 1870-1914*, London 1972, for more details and background.

5. Georges Sorel, 'Mes raisons du syndicalisme', *Matériaux d'une théorie du prolétariat*, Paris 1919, p.254.

6. See, for example, Aaron Noland, *The Founding of the French Socialist Party (1893-1905)*, Cambridge, Mass. 1956.

7. Sorel, 'Mes Raisons', *op. cit.* p.257.

8. *Ibid*. p.258.

9. Julliard, *op. cit.* p.113.

10. Georges Sorel, 'A propos d'anticléricalisme', *Études socialistes*, Vol.1(4), July-Aug. 1903, p.248.

11. Georges Sorel, 'Les polémiques pour l'interprétation du Marxisme (Bernstein et Kautsky)', *Revue internationale de sociologie*, April 1900, p.272.

12. *Ibid*. pp.278-79.

13. Georges Sorel, 'Conclusions aux "enseignements sociaux de l'économie moderne"', *Le Mouvement socialiste*, July 1905 pp.289-92.

14. Georges Sorel, *Le Décomposition du marxisme*, Paris 1908, p.34.

15. Sorel to Croce, 1 April 1898, p.13.

16. *Ibid*. 7 June, 1899, p.15.

17. Georges Sorel, *Réflexions sur la violence*, Paris 1908, p.46.

18. *Ibid*. pp.52-53

19. Georges Sorel, 'L'Église et l'état', *Cahiers de la Quinzaine*, series 3(3), 1901, pp.21-22.

20. Quoted in Robert Dreyfus, 'La Co-opération des idées', *La Revue blanche,* Vol.17, 1898, p.360.

21. Sorel, 'L'Église et l'état', *op. cit.* p.68.

22. Georges Sorel, 'Léon XIII', *Études socialistes*, Vol.1, Sept-Oct. 1903, p.372.

4. The Revolutionary *Syndicats* and the General Strike / pp.64-87

1. Georges Sorel, 'L'Avenir socialiste des syndicats' (1898) *Matériaux d'une théorie du prolétariat,* Paris 1919, p.67.

2. Claude Willard, *Socialisme et communisme Français*, Paris 1967.

3. Michelle Perrot and Annie Kriegel, *Le Socialisme Français et le pouvoir*, Paris n.d. p.40.

4. Sorel, 'L'Avenir socialiste', *op. cit.* pp.65-67.

5. *Ibid*. p. 80.

6. *Ibid*. pp.285-86.

7. Pierre Angel, *Eduard Bernstein et l'évolution du socialisme Allemand*, Paris 1961.

8. Sorel, 'L'Avenir socialiste', *op. cit.* pp.65-67.

9. *Ibid*. p.74.

10. *Ibid*. p.110.

11. *Ibid*. p.113.

12. *Ibid*. p.101.

13. *Ibid*. p.101.

14. *Ibid*. p.114.

15. *Ibid*. pp.58-59.

16. *Ibid*. p.59.

17. *Ibid*. p.63.
18. *Ibid*. p.102.
19. Georges Sorel, 'Grèves et droit du travail', (1900) in Sorel, *Matériaux*, *op. cit.* p.398.
20. *Ibid*. pp.411-12.
21. *Ibid*. pp.399-400.
22. *Ibid*. p.407.
23. Sorel, 'L'Avenir socialiste', *op. cit.* p.123.

5. Embourgeoisement: The Politics of Culture in the Era of Monopoly Capitalism / pp.88-107

1. Lenin described the general process of embourgeoisement clearly in the eighth chapter of his *Imperialism*.
2. Karl Kautsky, 'Le Socialisme et les carrières libérales', *Le Devenir social*, May and June 1895, pp.105-6.
3. Georges Sorel, 'Superstition socialiste?', *op. cit.* p.749.
4. Sorel to Croce, 27 Dec. 1897, *op. cit.* p.52.
5. Georges Sorel, 'L'Église et l'état', *op. cit.* p.68.
6. See for example, Sorel, *Réflexions*, *op. cit.* p.77.
7. Sorel, 'Superstition socialiste?', *op. cit.* p.750.
8. Sorel, 'Matériaux d'une théorie', *op. cit.* p.146.
9. Georges Sorel, *Les Illusions du progrès*, Paris 1908, p.1.
10. *Ibid*. p.286.
11. Sorel, 'Superstition socialiste?' *op. cit.* p.750.
12. *Ibid*. p.751.
13. Sorel, *Réflexions*, *op. cit.* pp.175-76.
14. Georges Sorel, *La Décomposition du marxisme*, Paris 1908, p.12.
15. Sorel, 'Superstition socialiste?', *op. cit.* p.762.
16. Georges Sorel, *Introduction à l'économie moderne*, Paris 1903, pp.66-67.
17. Georges Sorel, 'Le Syndicaliste révolutionnaire', *Le Mouvement socialiste*, 1 and 15 Nov. 1905, pp.278-79.
18. Sorel to Delesalle, 19 July 1903, in Georges Sorel, *Lettres à Paul Delesalle, 1914-1921*, Paris 1947, p.105.
19. Sorel, 'Le Syndicaliste révolutionnaire', *op. cit.* p.280.
20. Sorel, *Réflexions*, *op. cit.* pp.264-66.
21. Sorel to Croce, 13 Aug. 1920, *op. cit.* p.193.
22. See, for example, Peter Gay, *The Dilemma of Democratic Socialism*, New York 1952, p.223, where the professor says that 'Marx was no irrationalist *à la* Sorel and never preached violence for its own sake.'
23. Sorel, *Réflexions*, *op. cit.* p.51.
24. *Ibid*. p.217.
25. *Ibid*. p.83.
26. *Ibid*. pp.99-101.
27. *Ibid*. p.379.
28. *Ibid*. p.383.

Index

Action Française 16
'agit-prop' 21
Algeria 6,7
alienation 7,8,104
Allende, S. 16
Althusser, Louis 2
analogues 26,27
anarchism 62,66,69,72
anarcho-syndicalists 46
Angel, Pierre 115n
anti-semitism 47
aristocracy of labour 96–98
atomism 29

Bergson, Henri 12,31,58
Bernstein, Eduard 40,51–53,71,90,
    98,104
Blanquism 56
Bolshevik revolution 17,40,100,
    102,106,109,110
Bonaparte, Louis Napoleon 4,20
Bonnet, Paul 10
'born criminal' 23
bourgeois ideology 18,19,103
bourgeois philosophy 34
bourgeois thought 10
Bourses du Travail 5,17,43,67
British trade unionism 64
British working class 98–100

Les Cahiers de la Quinzaine 93
capitalist ideology 28,62,77,84
capitalist polity 43,50,86
capitalist values 76
catastrophic revolution 53
Catholic Church 51,61
Charzat, Michel 14
Christianity 54
Church and State 11,93
'cinematics' 30
class struggle 11,12,13,28,31,38,39,
    43,46,53,54,56,58,62,64,68,71,81,
83,86,88,90,92,98,99,103–105,
    111
'classical marxism' 35,40
commodity fetishism 105, 109
communards 4,65
Commune (Paris, 1871) 65
consciousness 41,46,49,54,57–59,
    71,72,76,83,91,93–95
consumption 101
co-operatives 74,75,78,95
Corsica 6–8
'counter-cultural' 1
counter revolution 22,73,95
criminal anthropology 23
'critical theory' 29
Croce, Benedetto 35,36,93,101,
    114n,115n,116n
culture: bourgeois 58,86,99,104,
    110; proletarian 33,74,76,79,88,
    102
Curtis, Michael 14,113n

David, Marie 8
Debray, Régis 111
Delesalle, Paul 17,100,106,116n
democratic centralism 5,110
determinism 29,37,38,40,41,62,70
Le Devenir social 10,25,52,92
Deville, Georges 10
dialectical method 27
dialectics 12,29,44
direct action 70–72, 81
'*diremption*' 12
Dreyfus Affair 11,44,46,48,50,59,
    62,72,94,100
Dreyfus, Alfred 11,47,49,51
Dreyfus, Robert 115n
Durkheim, Emile 9,22,24,25,27,28

Ecole normale supérieure 18
Ecole Polytechnique 6
economic determinism 12,35,52

'economic materialism' 35
'élan vital' 58
embourgeoisement 18,88–91,98–102,105,109,110,116n
empiricism 29,30
Engels, Frederick 18,48,51,61,66, 69,109; *Socialism: Utopian and Scientific* 55
England 54,79
L'Ère nouvelle 9,10
evolutionism 23

factory occupations 111
Fanon, Frantz 16,103,113n
fascism 13,15,16,105
fatalism 54,61,69,70,101
'force' 102
France 79,104
Franco-Prussian War 4,6,65
French Communist Party 106,109
French Philosophical Society 35, 101
French Revolution 20,33
French Workers' Party (*Parti Ouvrier Français*) 47,48,66
Freud, Sigmund 31

Gay, Peter 116n
General Confederation of Labour (*Confédération Générale de Travail* – C.G.T.) 5,17,43,67,106
general strike 55,57,58,64,79,80, 81; in France, 1968 111
German Social Democratic Party (SPD) 51,64
Germany 51,104
Goldberg, Harvey 113n
Gramsci, Antonio 1,13,17,60,89, 110,113n
Guesde, Jules 14,41,47,48,51,66, 98,104

Haymarket Affair 65
Hegel, G.W.F. 2,36
'hegelian revival' 2

'hegemony' 41,60,89,110
Henry, Emile 21
historical materialism 10,16,18,32, 35,37,53,69,86
Horowitz, Irving 113n
Hughes, H. Stuart 113n
l'Humanité 106
Humphrey, Richard 113n

idealism 29,30
Industrial Workers of the World (I.W.W.) 65
'infrastructure-superstructure' 26
integration, social and cultural 41, 85,89
intellectual: organic 17; revolutionary 2,17,58,106,110; socialist 62,68,70,73,110
International Socialist Congress (1889) 66

Jacobin democracy 59
Jaurès, Jean 14,18,41,47–49,100, 104
Julliard, Jacques 14,113n,115n

kantianism 34
Kautsky, Karl 10,51,90,92,104, 116n
Kent State University 21
Kriegel, Annie 115n

Labriola, Antonio 13,35,114n
Lafargue, Laura 66, 105
Lafargue, Paul 10,52,93,105
Lagardelle, Hubert 105
laissez faire 84,94,97
Latin America 111
LeBon, Gustave 9,22,24,58
Lefebvre, Henri 2
Lenin, V.I. 1,15,18,31,90,97,105, 106,109,114n,116n; *Imperialism* 90,109,114n,116n; *Materialism and Empirio-Criticism* 31
leninism 16,109

LePlay, Frédéric 19–21,24
LePlayists 25
liberal ideology 44
libertarian marxism 110
Lindenberg, Daniel 14,113n
'*lois scélérates*' 21
Lombroso, Cesar 9,23,24
Lukacs, George 1
Luxemburg, Rosa 1,49

McMahon, General 4
McManners, John 114n
Malthus, Thomas 26
maoism 111
Marcuse, Herbert 16,101,113n
Marx, Karl 1,9,10,12,18,30,32,34,
    36,37,39,48,51,52,54,56,57,69,70,
    71,76,86,97,104,109,116n;
    Capital 10; *The Communist
    Manifesto* 56,61; *The Economic
    and Philosophical Manuscripts
    of 1844* 30; *The German
    Ideology* 36,104; *The Poverty of
    Philosophy* 32
May Day 21,65,66
Meisel, James 113n
middle classes 43,44,50,59,60,63,
    105
Millerand, Alexandre 48
milieu 26,27
MIR (Movement of the
    Revolutionary Left) 16
Le Mouvement socialiste 105
Mussolini, Benito 16
'mutual aid' 74,75
'myth' 55,57,58

national traditions 54
Die Neue Zeit 92
New Left 1,14,88,111
Nietzsche, Friedrich 13
Noland, Aaron 115n

'objectivity' 24,25

organic-mechanical 10
organismic theory 26

Parnee, Douglas 113n
parliamentary socialism 68,71,72,
    80,91,94,103
Peguy, Charles 16,93,105
Pelloutier, Fernand 17,49,74
Perrot, Michelle 115n
phenomenology 29
Plekhanov, George 1,10,13
popular universities 60
positivism 31
Poulantzas, Nicos 2
praxis 41,48,68,69,88
'pre-sociology' 20
proletarian consciousness 2,89
proletarian revolution 51,80,87,94
proletarianisation 105,109,111
propaganda by the deed 21,72
Proudhon, Pierre-Joseph 32,33,34,
    114n

Radical Party 44,47,59
'radicalism' 44,49,60
rationalism 31,95
Ravachol 21
reformism 40,85,95,108
'Republican Defence' 48
Reuleaux, Franz 30,31,32,34,114n
revisionism 18,40,44,51,52,53,56,
    62,71,98
Revolution of 1848 4,20
revolutionary consciousness 12,31,
    34,38,48,51,67,72,73,81,85,95,
    101,102,104
revolutionary syndicalism 17,18,
    56,64,65,67–69,73–76,86,100,105,
    108,110,111
Revue communiste 106,107
Roth, Jack 15,113n
Rousseau, Jean-Jacques 77
Russia 79
Russian Revolution of 1905 100

sabotage 72
Sartre, Jean-Paul 2,16,113n
scientific socialism 55
Second Congress of Workers'
 Syndicats (1887) 65
Second Empire 7,19,33
Second Socialist International
 18,106
secularism 93
'self-management' 78
'Seize Mai' 4
social alienation 23,24
social liberalism 44,49,60,63
social pacifism 71,73
social science 19,99
Socialist Congress at Troyes
 (1888) 65
sociology 9,22–24,27–29,41,42,50,
 71,88,89,93,103
Sorel, Georges: and development
 of French marxism 1–3; life
 and intellectual formation
 4–12; interpretations of 13–
 16; on the revolutionary
 intellectual 16–18,110; and
 bourgeois sociology 19–28;
 epistemological orientation 29–
 32; influence of Proudhon
 32–34; on historical
 materialism 35–38; on theory
 and practice 39; contribution
 of 41–42; on political culture
 44–46,59,61; on socialist
 strategy 46–56,62,63; on Marx
 56,57; on 'Myth' 57,58; and
 revolutionary syndicalism 64–
 69,74–76,108,111; on direct
 action 70–72; 'social pacifism'
 73; the syndicats 77,78,87; on
 the general strike 79–81; on
 proletarian culture and
 embourgeoisement 88–91,94–
 96,98–102,104,109; on violence
 102,103; on Lenin and
 Bolshevik Revolution 106; The
 120

Decomposition of Marxism
 113n,115n,116n; Illusions of
 Progress 95,113n,116n;
 Introduction to Modern
 Economy 99,116n; Reflections
 on Violence 12,13,93,102,103,
 105,106,115n,116n; La
 Revolution dreyfusienne 49
Soviet Union 110
stalinism 110
Stanley, John L. 113n,114n
statism 11
strikes 82–85,102
student riots 21
'Superstition socialiste?' 10
syndicats 64,68,69,75,77,78,85,87

Tarde, Gabriel 9,22,24,58
terrorism 11,67,72,102
theory and practice 29–32,38,39,
 70
Third French Republic 4,7,65
trotskyism 110
Trotsky, Leon 1

'unionism' 75
United States 88,89,110,111
utopian socialism 53,55

Vaillant, Auguste 21
violence 102
voluntarism 54

Waldeck-Rousseau, Réné 45,114n
'welfare state' 101
Willard, Claude 115n
'workerism' 46,64,71
working class autonomy 5,64,67,
 71,74,75,78,84,106
'working men's clubs' 60
World War One 9,15,18,40,41,67,
 74,93,101,102,105,106,109
World War Two 13,111

Zola, Emile 19,23,47,49